Spotlights & Shadows

The Albert Salmi Story

Other Books by Sandra Grabman:

Plain Beautiful: The Life of Peggy Ann Garner

Pat Buttram, the Rocking-Chair Humorist

No Retakes! (co-authored by Wright King)

Spotlights & Shadows

The Albert Salmi Story

by Sandra Grabman
Foreword by Barry Newman
2nd Edition

BearManor Media
2010

Spotlights & Shadows: The Albert Salmi Story

© 2010 by Sandra Grabman.

For information, address:

BearManor Media
P. O. Box 1129
Duncan, OK 73534

bearmanormedia.com

Cover design by John Teehan
Typesetting and layout by John Teehan

ISBN—1-59393-425-4

Table of Contents

Acknowledgements

"I'm just prospectin' for the truth."

"There's your truth, from an eyewitness."

– Albert Salmi as the Sheriff
Bonanza, "Search in Limbo"

Many, many thanks to the following people, organizations, and publications for their help in providing the information and materials needed to put this book together:

Most of all to Albert's daughters, Lizanne and Jenny, for the generosity with which they shared their memories, photographs, and Albert's own handwritten memoirs—and to Albert himself, for being unselfish enough to start writing those memoirs at a time when life was becoming increasingly difficult for him. He must have felt compelled to reach out one last time to you, his highly-respected audience.

My gratitude to Jennifer Wilson, Albert's eldest granddaughter, for coming into my life and giving me information I didn't have before.

To those in the entertainment industry (actors, actresses, directors, producers, musicians, and playwrights) who shared their memories with us: Ed Ames, Lou Antonio, R. G. Armstrong, Tim Behrens, Harry Belafonte, Ruth Buzzi, Jack Carter, Veronica Cartwright, James Drury, Sonny Fox, Jack Garfein, J. E. Gessler, Peter Graves, Jonathan Harris, Richard Hayes, Pat Hingle, Claire Kirby Hooton, Russell Johnson, Wright King, S. L. Kotar, Nancy Malone, Dallas McKennon, Rod McKuen, Arthur Miller, Inge Morath, Bill Mumy, Patricia Neal, Barry Newman, Gloria Pall, Fess Parker, Dan Petrie Sr., Peter Mark Richman, John Saxon, William Shatner, George Shearing, Stella Stevens, Robert Sugarman, and Dennis Weaver.

To Albert's friends, relatives, neighbors and others for sharing their memories and knowledge with us: Elizabeth B. Anthony, Jeff Ballard, Wade Ballard, Sheldon Berger, Mary Calvert, Bill Carroll, Vince DeVito Sr., Vince DeVito Jr., Karen Dusik, Ray Dutczak, Eric Engberg, Ron Evans, Mark Galindo, Jim Garrity, Jean Greeley, Warren Hall, Elizabeth and Fred Hanson, Walt Hefner, Helen Hendrickson, Elaine Hill, Kathleen and Jake Jacobs, Stephen John Kalinich, Dr. Jerry and Linda Key, Jane Klain, Niilo Koponen, Dale Kriner, Eleanor LaFlamme, Brenda Laveck, Anders Lustig, Aune Luttio, Ivy Nevala, Nancy Paajanen, John Papanikolaou, Charles E. Rand, Eva Risnel, Elissa Della Rocca, Mark Rossmiller, Allen Salmi, Catherine Ann "Cassie" Salmi, Larry Simmons, Connie Stratton, Virginia Garner Swainston, Felicity Sweeting, Steve Tanner, Juha Terho, Simo Terho, Deane and Betty Tomlinson, Rev. Jerald Traeger, Beverly Vorpahl, Eila Vuorenmaa, Richard White, Yvonne Whiteley, and Marc Scott Zicree.

To these organizations and publications for their valuable information: The Actors Studio, the Duluth *Sunday News-Tribune*/Dick Kleiner, the Internet Movie Database, Lost in Space Australia, *The Los Angeles Times*, the Los Angeles Finlandia Foundation, *Modern Screen* magazine, the Museum of Television and Radio, the National Cowboy Hall of Fame, *The New York Times*, the Oregon Journal, the *Pioneer Press-Dispatch* [St. Paul], *Plays and Players* magazine, *Seura* magazine [Finland] and their writers Eero Kyllijoki and Risto Karlsson, *The South Middlesex News*, *The Spokesman-Review* [Spokane], *The Sun* [St. Paul], *The TV Collector*, and *TV Guide*.

FANS AND INTERNET POLL: Jeff Ballard, Chris Barnes, Janet Bell, Lisa P. Brzys, Jim T. Cholley, Jennifer, DeBost, Karen Dusik, Linda Ehlen, Klaus Haisch, Susie Hayes, Constance Isbell, Karen Mesterton-Gibbons, Kevin Petriello, Sarah Jane Richter, Alex Shiwan, Deanie Smith, Zane Stein, Marcia Studley, and Wanda Weidemann.

EDITORIAL HELP: Klaus Haisch, Linda Konner, Ben Ohmart, Laura Wagner, Matt Weimer, James Wilson.

HELP IN LOCATING PEOPLE: Fred T. Beeman, Shirley Crick, Patricia Neal, Allen Salmi, and Norma Tillman.

TRANSLATION OF FINNISH SOURCES INTO ENGLISH: Ilkka Heikkila, Anders Lustig and Nancy Paajanen.

RESEARCH HELP: Eric Engberg, Klaus D. Haisch, Kathy Havrilesko, Bob and Lorri Lesher, Bill Morlin, Mary O'Hara, David Prescott, Robert Richardson, Christy Stevens, and Laura Wagner.

TRANSCRIPTION: Kathy Havrilesko.

VIDEOTAPED SOURCES: Jeff Ballard, Ron Evans, Klaus D. Haisch, Constance Isbell, Andrea Lopez, Sarah Jane Richter, Ron Schultz, and Jake Tanner.

BACKGROUND INFORMATION: Rev. Cecil Bolding, Jack Brackett (Chief of Police, retired), Jennifer DeBost, Larry Crissman RPh, Rev. Michael Gabby, Roy Grabman, Klaus D. Haisch, Constance Isbell, Rev. Ann Koopmann, Anders Lustig, Dave Mazor, Juri Nummelin, Rev. Marguerite Oetjen, Floyd D. P. Oydegaard, E. Robbins, Allen Salmi, Ellen Sasse, Larry Simmons, and Maxine Walker.

PHOTOGRAPHS: *Seura* magazine, Kathleen and Jake Jacobs, Sonny Fox Productions, Jeff Sillifant/Still Things, NBC, Florence Doyle, Helen Hendrickson, Mary O'Hara, Photofest, E. Robbins, Catherine Salmi, Jennifer Salmi, Lizanne Salmi, Deanie Smith, Suomen Kuvapalvelu Oy, Vince DeVito and the estate of Virginia Swainston.

SUPPORT: Bob and Lori Lee Lesher

BOOKS:
Combat! A Viewer's Companion to the Classic TV Series, by Jo Davidsmeyer
Good Grief, by Granger E. Westberg
Respect For Acting, by Uta Hagen
The Twilight Zone Companion, by Marc Scott Zicree

WEBSITES:
http://ReelClassics.com
http://www.imdb.com
http://www.nationalcowboymuseum.org
http://www.reunion.com
http://www.ndmda.org
http://afsp.org

Foreword

Albert Salmi was not who you think he was. He wasn't who most entertainment reporters think he was, either.

For the two years that we were working together on the television series *Petrocelli*, we got to know each other exceedingly well. Albert Salmi was a man in love. He simply adored his wife Roberta. He was so proud of her. When she did something hurtful, he would either forgive her or totally overlook it. We were filming six days a week in Arizona, 485 miles away from his family. Did he take advantage of the freedom that distance gave him? No way! He missed his wife and children, and arranged for them to stay in the hotel with him during the summer when school was out.

Albert was unquestionably the sweetest, warmest, gentlest man I have ever known. He was also a giant in his field. Among the character actors who kept the entertainment industry alive, Albert was one of the best. If you were a moviegoer and television-viewer any time between 1958 and 1990, you probably saw him a lot. Sometimes his characters made you angry; sometimes they made you feel good all over.

In real life, Albert Salmi could make you cry.

When I received that terrible telephone call, telling me that he had killed Roberta, then himself, I just couldn't believe it. Today, eleven years later, I'm still in shock. Albert was not that kind of person.

Now, after years of rumor and speculation, someone has cared enough about Albert to find out the truth and make it public. Now you will meet the Albert that his friends knew, and you'll understand why his death was such a shock to us.

"To know him is to love him."

– Barry Newman
2001

1

Introduction

What makes me very sad is the fact that the first thing people most often asked when they learned that I was writing Albert Salmi's biography is a variation of the same question: "What really happened on April twenty-third?" It's as if his previous sixty-two years of achievement were wiped out of their minds by the events of his final day. Why is that? Maybe it's because they were having trouble accepting what they think happened. Maybe we all were. Maybe there's a good reason for that.

I didn't know it at the time, but the shock and disbelief I felt when I first learned about his death was shared by Albert Salmi's friends and co-stars all over the world. Maybe he *was*, as often as not, the bad guy on TV, and maybe he *was* awfully convincing in those roles—but something deep inside told me that he was altogether different from that in real life. Murder-suicide, with Albert behind the gun? What on earth could have led to such a tragic end for a man who had so much going for him? When his name came up after the tragedy, people would just shake their heads sadly. Was his life really that bad, I wondered? Didn't he experience any happiness at all? I had to find out.

Albert Salmi was one of the greatest character actors our country has ever produced. Because of that, most Baby Boomers easily recognized his face, but didn't know his name. That's because they saw him as his character, not as the actor. That's all the proof Albert needed that he was doing his job right.

Throughout my adolescence in the 1960s, I had seen this man in one Western after another. He rode a horse as though he had been riding one all his life. His Old West accent seemed completely genuine to my

Virginian ears. He seemed right at home hauling bales of hay and rounding up cattle. It looked so natural to see him in Western attire. Surely he must be a native of Arizona or thereabouts, I thought.

Then, I viewed the 1981 rebroadcast of *Bang the Drum Slowly* in which Albert and several other people involved with this 1956 production were interviewed. This time, he wasn't a character. He was appearing as himself—and the man was speaking with an accent that was distinctly New York. *New York?* After checking out biographical information about him, I discovered he was, indeed, born and raised in Brooklyn. That was the first of many surprises that would be revealed during the course of my research.

Albert was a favorite of casting directors. From 1955 until 1990, he was in over fifty movies and hundreds of television shows. Prior to that, he appeared on the live stage, and continued to do so occasionally throughout his life. The three types of roles he played most frequently on screen were those of the bad guy, the authority figure, and the misunderstood good guy. Albert was perfectly suited to either extreme—the bad guy, or the authority figure who arrests the bad guy. A brawny 6' 2", he could be quite intimidating when the need arose—and as loud and obnoxious as necessary to get the job done. Combine that with a couple days' growth of beard, uncombed hair, and maybe a dirty shirt, and voila! - there's your perfect bad guy.

On the other hand, his imposing size, authoritative voice, dominating presence, and confident manner also made him the perfect authority figure. *But* give him the role of a misunderstood good guy, and his voice would soften, his manner become less sure. The cold, hard stare of the bad guy would be gone; in its place would be gentle humility. His walk, talk, posture, facial expression, gestures, voice—everything was now different. Somehow, he no longer seemed quite as large. He was equally convincing in any role.

A method actor, he was able to project a huge range of genuine emotions that set him apart from ordinary character actors. So confident professionally, he was willing to take on roles of weakness—roles in which he cried, and many in which his character died. Once, he made his entrance in a wheelchair as the sweet-natured, mentally- and physically-disabled brother of the main character. When Albert played a victim, you could *see* the confused thoughts that were going through his mind. His pain was palpable.

Albert Salmi could have been a major star, but he intentionally carved out his career as a less-heralded character actor. In spite of that, he was given the lead a few times and he handled these roles like the pro he was. He never allowed his ego to get in his way. He played supporting roles with just as much energy and enthusiasm as he did leading ones.

His abundant energy was very much evident in one of his more off-beat characters—Alonzo P. Tucker, the pirate in two episodes of *Lost in Space*. This is a character that I didn't care for when, at age seventeen, I first saw him. He just didn't fit in with the macho image I expected of Albert at the time. Now though, viewing it from a more mature perspective over three decades later, Alonzo P. Tucker is my very favorite of all his characters (especially in the 1966 episode entitled "The Sky Pirate"). This character is tenderhearted and likable, though delightfully eccentric. It was a complete departure from any other character he had done, before or since. It combined human interest and science fiction with gentle humor. With his perfect timing, he did have a flair for comedy, even though he rarely got a chance to prove it.

Of course, a character actor's roles are quite diverse. I call Albert the "one-man trial" because he has played many of the people that one would find in a courtroom: judges, lawyers, criminals, victims, investigators, witnesses, spectators, and janitors. After watching him go from the role of a ruthless, cutthroat businessman to one of a sweet-natured paraplegic, casting directors seem to have realized that he could do anything; and they made good use of his versatility. There seemed to be no role too challenging for him.

During the course of my research I learned that he was admired by males and females alike. While he appealed to women, he was also a "man's man." He was the perfect balance of sensitivity and ruggedness.

After his stunning performance in his very first film, *The Brothers Karamazov* in 1958, MGM wanted to nominate him for an Oscar. Albert told them not to. Other awards *were* presented to him throughout his forty-year career, however. No one can say that his was not a very successful career.

So what was Albert Salmi really like? Was he as successful at home as he was on the screen? Did he have a lot of friends? What did he do when the cameras weren't rolling? If he was such a good man, why did he and his wife die so violently? And what was this connection with Finland that we keep hearing about?

There are many sources that state various facts about Albert and his work. Many of them are contradictory. Some hold him up as a saint, others as a monster. Which of these "facts" are real, and which are just rumor?

In researching Albert's life and talking with some of the people who meant the most to him, I have learned many surprising facts and have grown to respect the man even more—not only as a very gifted actor, but as a human being, as well. There was both triumph and tragedy in his life.

Let's travel the road together to see what led up to the worst tragedy of all—the gunshots that shocked the world.

– Sandra Grabman
2001

The Biography of
Albert Salmi

NOTE

Bold text indicates Albert Salmi's own recollections, taken from his unfinished, handwritten memoirs, written in 1990, and beginning, "This little book is of my experiences in theatre and films, which encompass some forty years." Even though I have taken the liberty of polishing up his first-draft writing a bit, the essence is entirely his. In addition to telling us about his career, these memoirs give us a rare glimpse of the mischievous little boy who grew up to become the ultimate character actor of his time. These are the happenings of his life, as he remembered them, from childhood until about 1970. Unfortunately, he did not live long enough to finish this project.

Chapter One

"The sheriff said decent folk respect decent ways."

Albert Salmi as George Breakworth
The Sweet Creek County War

In 1928, a postage stamp cost two cents. Amelia Earhart made headlines as the first woman passenger to fly across the Atlantic. Penicillin was newly discovered. And Calvin Coolidge was President of the United States.

Meanwhile, a Finnish couple was making news of their own in Brooklyn, New York. Svante and Ida Salmi had just become the proud parents of their first, and only, child, born on Sunday, March 11th, at Coney Island Hospital. Later in life, he would be known throughout the world as Albert, but on this day, they named him Alfred.

Little Alfred was in good company. Shirley Temple was born that year, as were Roddy McDowell, Fred Rogers, and James Garner. Mickey Mouse, in the classic *Steamboat Willie*, sprang to life in his first talkie, and the development of television was in its infancy.

Both of Alfred's parents had fled the civil war in Finland. The only world they had known, that of the Russian Empire, was now collapsing, so they came to America to seek a better life. The youngest of eight children, Ida Josefina Friman had been born and raised in Tampere, Finland. She had been a weaver there before immigrating to America to join her sisters Hilma ("Sanni") and Maria ("Alli") in 1920. Svante Salmi, formerly a lumberjack in Finland and now a carpenter, had come into America illegally through Canada in the 1920s. The couple married and settled in Brooklyn in 1924. Once Social Security legislation was passed, a change in jobs would become

Svante and Ida Salmi in the 1920s.
(Salmi family collection)

Ida proudly holding baby Alfred,
born on March 11, 1928.
(Helen Hendrickson)

routine whenever Svante's employer asked to see his Social Security card. He eventually obtained one, and his family enjoyed more stability.

The Salmis lived in an apartment building on Forty-First Street in the Finnish quarter in the Park Slope section of Brooklyn, and Finnish was their everyday language. The stoic, hardworking Finnish culture in which he was raised would have a powerful effect on Alfred throughout his life.

Svante was often away, going wherever his logging and carpentry services were needed. Ida's sister Sanni Sandstrom and her family, who lived in the same apartment building as the Salmis did, were good company for Alfred and his mother while his father was away. Sanni's daughter Helen was nine years older than her cousin. Little Alfred had never seen his grandparents. They—and most of his aunts, uncles and cousins—were still in faraway Finland. Later, he would yearn to see for himself his parents' homeland and get to know the relatives about whom he had heard so much throughout his childhood.

It became necessary for Ida to supplement the family income by working as a domestic housekeeper. Someone needed to take care of her two-year-old son while she was working, so she enlisted the help of Sanni's in-laws, Impi and Henry Sandstrom in Babylon, New York. The Sandstroms, like Ida, were from Tampere, Finland, and she felt a bond with them. They took young

Alfred in as a boarder during the summer. In this family, he no longer felt like an only child, for there were now three "brothers"—Arnold (age ten), Raymond (five), and Roy (four). Would a two-year-old child understand that this was only a temporary arrangement borne of necessity, that he was not being abandoned by his mother? It was only for a few months, however, and then he was back in Ida's arms. At age four, the need for long-term care again arose. This time, another branch of the Sandstrom family, Henry's brother Waino and his wife Adolfiina, lovingly cared for Alfred at their home in Fitchburg, Massachusetts. Their children were much older than he—Kaarlo was twenty-one and Irja Helen was seventeen—so Alfred found playmates in their neighborhood. It was there that he learned what would later be described as "fresh words" that he would use occasionally in the Sandstrom home. Most of the time, though, he behaved himself.

Even though Finnish was his primary language, Alfred couldn't quite pronounce its K sounds, so would substitute them with Ts. The Sandstroms thought it was so cute when he would ask for one of his favorite foods, hot dogs. In Finnish, two hot dogs are pronounced "kaksi makkarra." In Alfredese, however, it came out "tatsi mattaraa". After six weeks, he returned

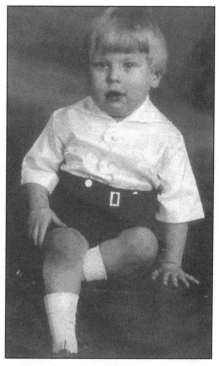

Little Alfred only spoke Finnish until he began school. *(Salmi family collection)*

Ida and Alfred. *(Salmi family collection)*

Albert and his cousin Helen.

Where he lived when he was 8.

They lived in a four-floor walk-up apartment on 41st Street in Brooklyn. *(Mary O'Hara)*

home to his parents.

Here, in his own words, is what his world was like back then:

Brooklyn was a simple place in my youth. The street on which we lived had quite an incline. In those days, apartment buildings were heated by hot water radiators and the furnace burned coal. Coal ash was put out every week in garbage cans. In the winters, with snow on the ground, we took the coal ash, put them on sleds and spread them at the bottom of the street. We did this to stop the sleds from going onto Fifth Avenue, a well-traveled street that also had trolley cars. The hill we sledded was between Fifth and Sixth Avenues on Forty-First Street, and every winter, many sledders were injured or killed by automobiles or trolley cars. The object was to get through the coal ash, safely cross Fifth Avenue, and then continue down to Fourth Avenue. To succeed was a thrill. Now, understand adults had nothing to do with the spreading of the ash. They made no attempt to control our dangerous endeavor. Maybe that's the best way. They let us make our mistakes without interference. We knew the dangers; we accepted them and tried to avoid them. Can you imagine what Social Services would do to parents today if this practice were still pursued?

Parents of that time and place were much less protective of their children than they are now, but that is not to say that Alfred's parents were neglectful. Svante, especially, was of the "old school" and was quite hard on his son. As was common back then, he ruled his family with an iron hand. Many years later, when talking to a friend about his father, Alfred described him as "a big, burly man who hung around taverns and got in fights." Albert told *The Sun* of St. Paul, Minnesota: "He was known to carry a knife. The Finns have a saying that means, 'I can take it all'— meaning the knife. My father was that kind of man."

Alfred's relationship to his mother, however, was more affectionate. From her, he learned tenderness.

Money was scarce for the Salmi family, as it was for their neighbors in the Great Depression. Still, Alfred and his buddies had devised ways to enjoy various forms of entertainment without the benefit of money:

The trolley cars mentioned earlier were also our mode of transportation, as we would jump on the back of them and ride as far as we wanted. When we desired to get off, we would simply pull a line that disengaged the electrical connection from the overhead line. The trolley car would stop and we would take off running. We were not favorites of the trolley operator because every time he would have to come to the back of the trolley and replace the connection so the trolley could proceed. In those days, we could travel all over Brooklyn by trolley—even to Coney Island, which we did a great deal.

"I remember the kids that hung onto the backs of the trolleys and busses to hitch a ride," says Larry Simmons, who was two years behind Alfred in their school. "Many of us did travel in groups that today would be frowned upon. You have to remember that things were a lot different then, and a lot tougher."

It was a simpler life.

In January, the Christmas trees were put out by the garbage. The streets had four-story apartment buildings from Fourth Avenue to Seventieth Avenue, so you can imagine how many trees there were. We would collect the trees until we felt we had enough—a large pile of Christmas trees. You can imagine the temptation. Why do youngsters love to set a fire? On Forty-First Street, there was a

Ida stayed home with Alfred during the summers. *(Salmi family collection)*

park, a small park, just across the street. Its boundaries were on Forty-First from Fifth to Seventh and from Forty-First to, I think, Forty-Fifth (between Park Slope and Bay Ridge). It was named Sunset Park. There was a six-foot stone wall encircling the park, with entrances at every corner. At any rate, we gathered these Christmas trees, put them in a large pile and set fire to them. Talk about tradition! We did it every year for years and years, and no police or city officials ever interfered.

Sunset Park had a public swimming pool. We never paid to enter. We preferred to climb a fence, with bathing suit and towel. We also never paid for going to the movies, always climbing in the window of the men's room in the back, or slipping in a side door when someone was exiting.

In Finland, families would go to Halls for companionship and entertainment, and the Salmis found such a place in New York. Ida and her son would frequently take the subway to the Fifth Avenue Hall in Harlem. One of the prime sources of entertainment there was stage plays, as Finns had a high respect for good acting. Of those few children's roles that had speaking parts, most went to young Alfred Salmi, his talent already recognized.

From Sixth to Tenth Avenues was the Finnish ghetto. I'm a Finn. I grew up there. In fact, when I first entered the public school system, I could speak no, or very little, English. I was told to go home and learn English and then, and only then, return for my education. There were no bilingual teachers in those days. I did it in short order and began my education, such as it was.

Where did he learn English?

"On the streets," answers his youngest daughter, Jenny. That method seems to have worked well.

The area from First to Sixth Avenue was the Italian ghetto, and from Tenth to Twentieth Avenue was the Jewish ghetto. We attended the same public schools through junior high. We mingled freely and made fast friends. But if one boy from one group did something to another boy from another group, there would be a gang fight. Oh, not like the gang wars of today. No. Ours consisted mainly of sticks and stones. Very seldom did anyone get seriously damaged.

Arnold Schuster was one of the Jewish boys. He gained fifteen minutes of recognition and was gone. Arnold recognized Willie Sutton, the infamous bank robber. His tip to the police resulted in Sutton's capture, trial and jail. Some misguided hoodlum, or perhaps friend of Sutton's, killed Arnold Schuster. The murderer was never found.

I had a short-lived experience as a Boy Scout, but wearing the uniform (and it was only a half uniform—shirt, Boy Scout tie and hat) meant a fight from one of the three groups, including my own. I got tired of fighting every time I put the uniform on, so I quit the Boy Scouts. I never got one merit badge. Why everyone disliked the Boy Scouts is something I have never been able to figure out.

My school was uneventful.

Nevertheless, Alfred was a smart boy and his command of English was quite good. He wrote to his cousin Helen in Minnesota when he was only eight:

Dear Helen,

Thank you for your letter. I was very glad to get it. I will try to answer it as well as I can.

I am eight years old, and as you said I am in the third grade. No, I don't like to go to school but I have to go.

What do you do in summer? We have three pools in the park. One a wading pool, one a very deep diving pool, and the middle pool is the swimming pool which is 3 feet deep.

Yes, my mother does still go to work. Not so much in the summer as in the winter.

How old are you? Do you like school? How many more years do you have to go to school before you are finished with school? What are you going to do when you are all through with school?

This is all for this time.

Good Bye.

Alfred

P.S. I will wait for your letter. So long.

Written in Finnish at the end of this letter is a note from his mother, Ida. Translated, it says: "Hello, Helen and Alli. Alfred was very happy to receive the letter. He read it all by himself very eagerly. It was the first time he received a letter addressed directly to him."

Those long separations earlier must have taken their toll since Ida now opted to stay home when school was out for the summer instead of sending her son to live with friends while she worked.

It appears that it was important to her that Alfred would be able to dress nicely when the need arose. Even though times were hard and money tight, she scraped up enough to buy Alfred a nice suit and tie.

Young Albert Salmi.
(Helen Hendrickson)

I walked to public school and I walked to junior high school. Then my life started changing. I was interested, as a youth, in aviation and though there were academically good high schools in Brooklyn, Manhattan and Queens, I opted for Haaren High because it was an aviation trade school.

"Haaren was located in Manhattan on Tenth Avenue and took the whole block between Fifty-Eighth and Fifty-Ninth Streets on the west side of Tenth," says fellow student Larry Simmons. "Haaren disbanded in the late 1970s."

In three and a half years, the closest I got to aviation was the World War I Spad they had on exhibition in a large room on the ground floor of the annex building on the east side of Manhattan in Harlem.

Simmons continues, "I also went to Haaren for the aviation course. It was a theory course."

I didn't realize when I picked Haaren that it was a trade school for the academically poor student who could get into no other high school in New York. Though enrollment was predominately black, with whites being the minority, there were never any race problems at the school. Any fights that erupted on school grounds were settled one on one, generally as fistfights. I don't remember a great deal about the school except that I learned, in shop, to make a pretty good, efficient "zip gun" that actually fired a twenty-two-caliber bullet. I learned to watch my overcoat. In winter, if you looked out the window, you could see overcoats dropping from floors above to waiting conspirators below. I played a lot of "hooky."

"Cutting classes was a natural pastime at Haaren for many. I did it myself a bit, mostly in the middle two years," says Simmons. "I personally can't think of anyone who got caught. However, if they did, I would think that they would have gone to see Dr. Mantell, the Dean. He was good training for meeting my D.I. when I went into the USMC".

While I was in high school, I went into the Golden Gloves. I won the first fight. The second fight was with a fellow connected with P.A.L. (Police Athletic League). He knew more than I did about the finer points of boxing. He beat my brains out!

Then, life changed for Alfred Salmi at age sixteen:

I had broken the law and had been caught. I suppose I should explain how I broke the law.

We had a way of making money in those days, along Fifth Avenue in Brooklyn. We would wait at a stoplight. When a truck stopped for the red light, one of us would swing aboard and throw out of the

Albert at Haaren High School.
(Salmi family collection)

back whatever the truck was hauling, a confederate would pick up the boxes and at the next red light, the truck boarders would dismount and go back to see what wondrous things were in the boxes. If we liked what we found, we'd keep it; but generally, we fenced it. It was safer to sell it than keep it. Nowadays, if you notice, the back of all trucks are closed and locked. Yes, it was a simpler time.

The day dawned and went badly for me. I was caught on a truck after having tossed off the packages. It was, for me, jail or farm work. The war was on. Because I took farm work, I was given a high school diploma, which was sent to my parents' home in Brooklyn. I never went back to [public] school.

I spent two summers in Vermont on a dairy farm as a general farm hand, hand milking cows, bringing in the hay, putting it into the hay mow, slopping the pigs, keeping varmints down. [Later, he would play characters who performed farm chores as if he had been doing that for years.] I shot a lot of groundhogs and fed them to the hogs. The farmer fed me popcorn and only popcorn on Saturday night because he said I didn't need energy for Sunday because I didn't work Sunday.

Another codicil to my arrest was the extraction by the officials of my promise to join the military. It seemed like an acceptable bargain.

Another, even more traumatic event occurred when Salmi was seventeen. On May 18, 1945, his father had come home from work that evening feeling quite ill, and informed his family that he was going to die. They took him to Kings County Hospital, where he succumbed that very night of pneumonia that had caused his chronic heart problems to turn fatal. At only fifty-three years of age, Svante Salmi was dead.

Being now the only English-speaking member of his family made it necessary for Alfred to handle many family matters. He served as interpreter for his mother when needed, and worked with the funeral director and signed his father's Certificate of Death as its informant.

According to family legend, Svante was such a large man they had used a piano box as his coffin and, even then, had a difficult time closing the lid. Two men had to sit on the lid in order to close it. The absurdity of that situation struck Alfred as funny. Knowing that it was socially unacceptable to laugh at his own father's funeral, though, he stifled it as much as he could. (Decades later, when he related this story to friends, Albert broke out into joyous laughter, feeling free now to enjoy the humor of the situation. He laughed so long and hard that tears came to his eyes.)

Even though Alfred had often been teased about the similarity between his name and the word "salami," he stubbornly held on to it. After all, it was evidence of his proud, Finnish heritage. Alfred did, however, change his first name. His schoolmates had called him Albert, and he came to prefer it; so he had it officially changed. He obtained his Social Security number under that name shortly before his eighteenth birthday.

Looking back on his youth many years later, he told his daughters that it seemed that all of his childhood friends ended up either in jail or dead. He seemed to be one of the few who made something of himself. Perhaps being caught while still young, then being given the structure and discipline of farm work and the military, was the best thing that ever happened to him.

At age eighteen, Albert went into the U.S. Army on May 7, 1946. Three weeks later...

I was sent to Annisten, Alabama, for basic infantry training. That was a new world to me. In this stream of consciousness, it occurs to me that I was a scrapper, something I never considered myself to be. I've always thought that I was a lover. I had sex with four girls. I probably had ten fights.

After basic training, he was assigned to the 7706th AFN Company, APO 75. His powerful physique led to his being made a military policeman and stationed in Europe. It was while serving as MP that he developed a strong distaste for firearms.

Albert in the Army, with Uncle Kalle and Aunt Lilli Jalmari. *(Salmi family collection)*

One of his MP duties was to guard visiting stars Linda Christian and Tyrone Power, who were there on tour. He realized that he would really enjoy going on such a tour, and it wouldn't be particularly hazardous. He was told he had to audition, which he did, and he was reassigned as announcer and engineer with the tour. This was much better than police work.

While stationed in Germany in 1947, he had been given a twelve-day leave, with permission to visit the western zones of Germany, France and England, but he really wanted to visit his parents' homeland, Finland. His Uncle Kalle Jalmari and his wife Lilli were somewhat taken aback to discover a police officer at their door late that night, but their shock quickly turned to joy when they realized who this young soldier was, and that the policeman was merely an escort.

Salmi visited his cousins Eila Vuorenmaa, Paavo Terho and Paavo's brother Jaakko, again in 1985 in Helsinki, and they reminisced about this earlier visit:

"Do you still recall what you especially asked for when Mom asked for your favorite dish?" Eila, daughter of Kalle and Lilli, asked.

"Now let me see," Albert mused. "I'm pretty sure I said I wanted meatballs."

Meat was rationed back then, but nothing was too good for Ida's son. Eila tells with fondness of the letters and packages of food and clothing that they had received from her aunts and their families in

America during wartime. Ida and her sisters had been separated from their family by an ocean, but love and concern had kept them all united in spirit.

American soldiers were quite rare in Finland in 1947, and many people in town didn't believe that Albert was one because he could speak Finnish. It was a language that was difficult for a non-Finn to learn, so they would never expect an American soldier to know it.

During his stay, nineteen-year-old Albert Salmi, with energy to spare, went dancing at the best dancing spots in Pispala—the Workers' Club Concert Hall and the Volunteer Fire Department Hall. He had a lot going for him—good looks and a snappy uniform. He even met a girl there and took her out on a date a few days later.

His Uncle Kalle took him to see the Finlayson textile mill, where Albert's mother had worked as a weaver many years before; and his fourteen-year-old cousin Simo proudly showed him the house in Tampere where Ida and her family had lived.

Remembering his happy times on stage at the Fifth Avenue Hall back in New York, and perhaps having been influenced by Linda Christian and Tyrone Power, Albert had a pretty good idea what he wanted to do with his life. "He was dreaming of a career as a film star and had great hopes for the future," his cousin says. He had heard of an acting school in Norway and was considering going there for a while.

The German currency he carried were negotiable only near his unit in Germany, and he soon found them worthless in Finland, so his relatives ended up financing his visit and return flight home. He never forgot their generosity.

He had had an enjoyable visit with his mother's relatives, and hoped to someday come back to Finland to visit his father's side of the family. He then returned to his unit in Germany, apparently never being caught for going to the forbidden country.

During his military career, Albert achieved the grade-four level of Sergeant and received the World War II Victory Ribbon, World War II Victory Medal, Army of Occupation Medal and Lapel Button. On May 18, 1949, he was given an honorable discharge at Camp Kilmer, New Jersey.

Some big decisions lay ahead.

Chapter Two

"I want to get some learnin'. I want to go to school."

Albert Salmi, as Raif Simmons
The Virginian, "A Little Learning"

Fresh out of the Army and back in New York, Salmi found that most of his friends had moved away, and he considered his options. He definitely did not want to go back into farm work; he'd had enough of that to last a lifetime. Instead, he took a job as a uniformed guard with the William J. Burns International Detective Agency. It certainly wasn't his dream job, but at least it provided an income. When the agency asked him to start carrying a gun, however, he quit.

An honorable discharge from the military meant he was eligible for the GI Bill. With this, he could get education in the career of his choice. This was his chance to fulfill his dream. According to an article about him in the March, 1967 issue of *TV Guide*, it happened this way: "One day while strolling down a street in his native New York after Army service, he saw a sign for a new theater workshop. 'Right there I decided to study acting under the GI bill,' he says. 'It actually was a form of goldbricking, I suppose. There would be no tests and no homework, but I still could collect $75 a month.'" He later admitted to a second motive, as well. "How do I meet girls? The government will pay if I go to dramatic school. That's where all the girls are," Albert said with a grin. "So I went to dramatic school."[1] Thus began his love affair with the stage, which would provide a healthy outlet for his powerful emotions. His education began at Erwin

---

[1] *The Spokesman-Review*, "Acting became his life and love", by Beverly Vorpahl (6/17/84).

23

A civilian once again. *(Salmi family collection)*

Piscator's Dramatic Workshop, then at the American Theater Wing. It was there and, in 1951, the Actors Studio that he learned his craft.

It wasn't all work and no play, however. Actress Gloria Pall recalls, "Albert and I both went to the Dramatic Workshop back in 1948. We hung out together, went to see Broadway shows, walked for miles along Broadway gathering snow flurries in the winter and suntans in the summer."

I was fortunate to work with Mr. Erwin Piscator (the noted German director). He was a theatrical man of no small genius. His exploits in theatre were legendary before he started the Dramatic Workshop on Forty-Eighth Street, just off Eighth Ave. He worked originally in Hitler's Germany and, when war broke out, he re-established himself in Russia. His reputation preceded him, and the Russian government gave him carte blanche. His claim to glory in Russia was a period war picture, which he directed. The Russian government gave him a battleship but didn't realize that he was going to blow it up and sink it. When he did it, on film, the Russians were aghast. They expelled him, but not before he had gotten the half-finished film out of the country. I'm sure that he wanted to finish it somewhere else, but he never succeeded in doing it. I never saw a frame of the film, but it must have been incredible.

This man I studied with—he was not a "method director," as most of the teachers I worked with later, but his technique was infallible. What Piscator did was to show the fledgling actor exactly what to do, when to pause, when to deliver the line, by example. He would demonstrate and then have the actor do it, over and over again until he was satisfied. By this repetition, the young actor (and that was all of us) came to understand the effect of the acting. It became second nature and very clean.

It also helped to see him work with other actors because then you were far enough away from the action to make your own judgment as to what was occurring. Generally, one marveled at the accuracy of the emotion "indicated" by the actor involved. This form of teaching I eventually got away from but, for a foundation, it was invaluable.

"Indicating" emotions for a professional actor is death. For a beginning actor, it is a good form if one can make the distinction. Stella Adler was good at this form of teaching, as was Piscator. Her students were easy to pick out when they acted, because they all indicated emotions and did it well, but they never soared.

The Dramatic Workshop instilled a sense of crusade in the actor. When one performed at the workshop, it was as if one took on a clerical collar or the position of a teacher. The actor wanted the audience to recognize an unsavory character as truthfully as he could, so that any audience seeing it would be repelled by that individual and vow never to be like him. If one person left a performance saying, "I will never be as bad as that character was," the actor felt fulfilled. If the person left the theatre better than he entered it, we felt we were accomplishing something. The reverse was true, too. If one in the audience saw and believed the goodness in the human condition and sought to emulate this behavior, we, the actors, felt a warm sense of accomplishment. Sometimes, people would come backstage in these amateur school productions and state in an oblique way that they were better people for seeing the production. This was better than any award an actor could get, and still is!

There were five or six of us actors who became disciples of this priestly/teaching condition, and we pursued it diligently. There was a bar/saloon directly across the street from the school and, though

Albert in the Actors Studio, 1951.

we were on short rations (the GI Bill offered few luxuries), we would assemble in a back room of the bar, order a few pitchers of beer and improvise on situations we dreamed up. The hour went by quickly and our imagination, so important to actors, was exercised almost daily. The patrons of the bar were our audience, and they enjoyed our endeavors. Sometimes, they passed the hat for us; sometimes they didn't. This very act was a barometer as to how successful we were. It was a form of comillia del arte that the Italians practiced, wherein the audience would suggest a situation, a place, and the characters, and the actors would then produce a theatrical piece from their suggestions. It was an exciting time and we discussed theatre and acting constantly. We were living pure theatre and growing in the process. This adventure was constant for a few years, always coupled with the class work across the street.

The owner of the bar had a special place in his affection for actors. Every Christmas, he gave us drinks on the house if we decorated his bar with garlands and all the trappings of Christmas. He provided all the materials and we put them up. It was interesting to see the final product, and it was always commented on. We started out in an efficient manner, but at the end of the decorating, it appeared as if some demented monkeys had thumbtacked the decorations in no special plan. Progressively, the free drinks affected our judgment. It still had a kind of charm, if not a measured charm.

Salmi had taken an entire year off from full-time work in order to focus his energies on learning. While studying at the American Theatre Wing, he ushered in the evenings at the Alvin Theatre. Working there turned into a learning experience, too, observing the great actors of the day.

They didn't see Albert as character-actor material in those days, instead, grooming him as a leading man. In the 1953 Players' Guide (*The Annual Pictorial Directory for Stage, Screen, Radio and Television*, sponsored by the Actors' Equity Association and American Federation of Television and Radio Artists), he was listed under the heading "Young Leading Men."

I did some leads in plays at the workshop for invited audiences at the school. The workshop had a real theatre downtown and that's where the larger productions were mounted, and we had a paying audience. We, the actors, weren't paid; but the school did generate some revenue.

There in that theatre, a large production, The Burning Bush, was mounted. It was, as I remember, about a youngster who witnesses the legendary burning bush and is given supernatural powers. The authorities seek to discredit him and put him on trial for his life. (The actor [Jack Garfein] who played the youngster is now the head of a theatre in New York that he established in about the early eighties. [Salmi is probably referring to The Actors and Directors Lab in New York City. Garfein now also runs Le Studio in Paris.] **He was a survivor of the Nazi concentration camps and to this day has the serial numbers tattooed on his arm. He was well accustomed to tragedy, fear, and survival. He played his role magnificently.)** It was a one-set play, the set being a massive courtroom. The judge was sitting stage right on an eight-foot elevated bench; underneath directly in front of the bench were secretary, bailiff, and court reporter. Center stage was a witness box, which was on rollers and was moved readily around the stage. Upstage were twelve jurors, leaning to the prosecutor. Stage left were the spectators. Piscator (who directed it) believed in the living theatre and involved the audience not only through the play, but he also had the subpoenaed witnesses scattered and sitting in the audience, so that when they were called, they came from the audience onto the stage and into the witness box. I had been cast as one of the witnesses, along with Raikin Ben-Ari. As two hapless fishermen who had witnessed the boy and the burning bush, we were threatened and badgered by the government, the court and the prosecution. So as we went up to testify, we were two frightened witnesses.

Incidentally, Raikin Ben-Ari was also a drama teacher at the school. I felt particularly honored to work so closely with an accomplished actor. Ben-Ari also had left Germany just before the war broke out. He had been a highly-regarded actor in the Jewish theatre there. Well, we were called and down the aisle we came, climbed the stairs to the stage, and entered the witness box. The prosecutor was relentless, the questions came fast and furious, and we got more frightened and more confused as the scene progressed. Our confusion was so rampant that the spectators (actors) on stage broke into laughter. At this point, the judge banged his gavel, once, twice, and the third time the head of the gavel came off. The handle bounced off the judge's bench, fell and hit the stenographer, seated below, smack on the head. An accident. I broke and started laughing, trying the whole while to appear to be crying instead of laughing. I was having a difficult time pulling it off.

Then it happened. Raikin Ben-Ari stamped on my foot as hard as he could. My laughter turned immediately to pain and then tears. He saved a difficult situation and made my indicated tears to real tears, and I felt, for the first time, a true emotion on stage. It was a revelation! I tried to do it in subsequent performances and found it difficult, if not impossible. There was the fault in the Piscator school of acting. The actor must not indicate emotion, but must find, through his instrument, how to bring forth true, genuine emotions. This was the path I wished to travel but knew nothing about how to do it. I didn't even know if it was taught. I thought, perhaps, only talented geniuses could bring forth this wonderful feeling of true emotions on stage.

"I loved him very much," says Jack Garfein of Salmi. After *The Burning Bush*, he directed him in a play called *Squaring the Circle* about Soviet Russia. This was one of the first plays Garfein ever directed, and he wanted Albert in it. Then, when it came time to do his first big production, entitled *End As a Man*, Garfein wanted him in that, too.

Garfein feels that, at this stage of his career, Salmi was something of an outsider. Garfein could relate to that, having come from the war and being alone in New York. "It created a kind of a bond between us," he said. As an actor, though, he felt that Albert "had an authenticity on the stage that was not actor-y. There was nothing actor-y about him. It was a reality. He was on the stage and your imagination was stirred by his background, his life. You didn't feel that he came from a theatrical, sophisticated background, but you sensed the background with a certain kind of a rustic life behind it."

Before I leave the subject of the Dramatic Workshop, I'll relate one more happening. One afternoon, I was sitting on a stool at the Footlight Bar and in comes a fellow actor. He sat down on the stool next to me and, after a bit of small talk, he said that he was going to try a singing career because there just weren't enough roles for black actors. He was quite right. Back in the late forties and early fifties, there was no work for the black actor. The situation has not gotten much better in forty years. There has been improvement; there should be more. Anyway, this actor did as he said he would and has gone on to international recognition. [Harry Belafonte was a student of the Dramatic Workshop at the same time as Albert and was acquainted with the Footlight Bar, so he is probably the gifted singer/actor that Albert is remembering here.]

Early publicity photo. *(Claire Kirby Hooton)*

Salmi took every class he could, spending sixteen hours a day honing his skills. He took speech, voice, projection, even fencing lessons for four years, becoming an expert fencer in the process. Before he knew it, the theater had become more than just a way to meet girls or a free ride financed by the GI Bill—it had become his life. He was very much influenced by the philosophy of that time and place, believing that screen work was exceedingly inferior to stage work. Those who crossed the line were considered turncoats. So he spent the first part of his career doing stage work and live TV, stubbornly resisting the temptation to break into movies.

Life was becoming more complicated and demanding now, and Albert sometimes yearned for the simple life, again. He had a fantasy - he wanted a sloop of his very own. In order to make this fantasy a reality, he thought that he could work a couple jobs and save up the $7,500. He could then buy his sloop and spend the next two years just sailing. Such a simple, peaceful life would be utopia.

"Making rounds"—that is going to agents' and producers' offices—daily is something every actor in New York did in the forties and fifties. The cutthroat aspect of the theatre was non-existent. All actors and actresses were comrades of hard times. If, for instance, I heard of a job and went to see about it and did not get it, I would seek out one of my actor friends who I thought would be perfect for the role and tell him about it. They did the same for me.

One day, I was making the rounds with another actor and was at the agent's office. The agent's office always had an inch of dust in it, his shirt was always dirty and his tie spotted, but he got jobs for actors. How he did it, I'll never know. On this day, in this agent's office, was a producer of a small summer stock company. The other actor and I read a little for him, selecting pieces from the ten plays to be done that summer. We were hired on the spot and told to take the train to the town where the stock company was located. Ten weeks of work! We were walking down Broadway when it occurred to me that I didn't want to go to this job. I don't remember if we'd signed a contract or not. I think we didn't sign one and that's why I was hesitant to go. We ran into an actor who was some four inches shorter than I and going prematurely bald. I told him about the job and I said I wasn't interested in going. I asked him if he would go in my place. He mentioned the fact that he was shorter and balder than I. I countered by saying that the producer only saw me for some half-hour and has probably forgotten what I look like. That short, bald actor went to that summer stock company and did the ten shows. The only difficult moment he had was the first work morning when the producer said he didn't look like the actor he'd seen in New York, but then he had seen so many actors that he accepted the actor who substituted for me. I was going to the Dramatic Workshop at that

time and I really didn't feel I could give up the class work. The Dramatic Workshop was really the beginning of a work ethic.

There was another agent who primarily cast actors for Signal Corp films. These were all filmed up in Queens, New York. They were informational, for servicemen. At nine o'clock, actors filled up his outer office and waited. About 9:20 a.m., this agent would stick his head out of the door to his inner office, a room I never was privileged to see. He stuck his head out, looked around the room, and said, "you, you, you" as many as were needed. I was one of those "you's". The secretary took all information, name, social security number, address, etc., etc. We, the chosen, were given directions to the studio in Queens. We traveled by subway. Sitting in the subway car, we talked of our service experiences, we talked about work and the difficulty of getting it, we talked about the cheapest places in Manhattan to get a good meal, we talked about everything. When we got to Queens, the director assigned us our parts and the costumer gave us our uniforms.

I was given a uniform with corporal stripes, one of the actors a private, and three of the others became instant officers and gentlemen. Funny thing, I served thirty-six months in the U.S. Army, my highest rank being "buck sergeant". The training was still there. I found that these actors that I spoke to so freely on the subway became individuals whom I could not approach or talk to! The separation of enlisted man and officer was so instilled that it was impossible to ignore. I'd probably been out of the service for only about a year and a half. To this day, I can remember my serial number: 422-80-496. I don't know my car license number, sometimes I forget my telephone number—but never my serial number.

As I was coming to the end of my time at the American Theatre Wing, I began working on a scene from From Here to Eternity as an audition for The Actor's Studio.

There was a predominance of men at the Theatre Wing, due, in large part, to the GI Bill, so they often enlisted professional actresses when women were needed in their scenes. Salmi learned much about acting from these women, too, but was about to meet one who would teach him a lot more than acting.

The actress I chose was one of the volunteer professional scholarship actresses at the Wing. You would recognize her name. She has had a nice career and worked for a number of years on a series. This actress and I rehearsed very, very long hours for months. This was to be her audition also. As normal, we had a sexual relationship. She was marvelously wild and abandoned in bed, and also in her acting. We kept finding things in rehearsal and we never became bored. If the rehearsals lagged, we played around sexually. When we were tired sexually, we rehearsed—in my apartment, in her apartment (when her roommate was out), even on tables in rooms at the Theatre Wing. Finally, we got a date for the audition.

But (and what a but!) five days before the audition, my actress partner slashed her wrists in a suicide attempt! I discovered it as I was riding the subway home. It was a Saturday night and I had picked up the Sunday News. I was leisurely reading through it when a story heading caught my eye: "Actress (her name) attempts suicide by slashing wrists and has been taken to Bellevue for examination"!

Well, the next day was Sunday and there was no visiting on Sunday. Sunday went very slowly, and first thing Monday I was there at Bellevue. When I got there, I was informed that only family members were allowed to visit. I told them I was her fiancé and it was imperative that I see her as we were soon to be married. They finally ushered me into a room on the second floor.

As I entered the room, there she was, wrists bandaged, huddled in a corner. I didn't approach her immediately. I talked to her quietly and eventually I got close enough to take her hand gently. She said only one thing. She said please not to let them take her up to the third floor, because she would never get out of there if they did. I told her I would do everything in my power to get her released, though at that moment, I didn't know how I could accomplish it. While I was stroking her hand, I realized she had a crumpled paper clenched in her fist. Gently, ever so gently, I opened her hand, took the paper, and put it in my pocket. I was there a very short while, and soon I was asked to leave.

Once outside, I took the paper from my pocket and looked at it. It was a telegram from her agent saying he was sorry for her trouble, and he would do everything he could to help her. This was my cue for action. I immediately went to his office. He knew of me through her, so I had no difficulty in getting in to see him. Once inside his office, I blew up. I threw the telegram on his desk and told him to help her immediately or I'd throw him out the window. We were on the fourteenth floor. He asked me how he could do that. I told him that he must know of a psychiatrist who could talk to her and get her out of there. I was shaking with anger; he saw it, and he did make a phone call. I don't know who he called but his conversation led me to believe that she was going to be helped. I left the office.

I tried other avenues, to no avail, but then two days later her roommate called me to say she would be out the next day. She asked me to accompany her to Bellevue to fetch our girl. Naturally, I said yes.

The next day, I went to the apartment to pick up the roommate for our trip to Bellevue. On the way, I told her of the incident with the agent. She said that he had nothing to do with her release. It seems that when she went to see our girl, she met the head psychiatrist at Bellevue. After a conversation with him, she was allowed to see our girl. The psychiatrist called the roommate and told her that if she would go to bed with this roach, he would see to it that she was released. The roommate said she was too upset to think of sex while her friend was locked up but that, as soon as she was released, she'd give him the ride of his life. Our girl was released and the doctor called. The roommate lowered the boom on this sick character. She told him in every way possible what a scumbag he was and told him never to call her again.

To this day, I think these doctors of the mind need doctors of the mind need doctors of the mind. In other words, I think all psychiatrists are parasites who are incapable of helping anyone. Can you imagine the head of the Psychiatric Department at Bellevue being sicker than the people delivered to his care?

This incident had far-reaching effects. Decades later, Albert's refusal to seek professional help for his depression resulted in his final year of life being absolutely miserable, and likely contributed to his death.

She was out, and amazingly, in time for the Studio audition. She really wanted to do it and so did I. I wasn't sure if she was up to it, but I was ready to go ahead. We went to the Studio on the appointed day and waited for our turn to audition. We knew that beyond those doors to the audition room sat Lee Strasberg, Gage Kazan, and Cheryl Crawford, and only by unanimous vote would an individual pass. Out of perhaps two hundred auditions, perhaps one, sometimes two, sometimes more, were selected. The scene had to be five minutes. If it went over five minutes, you were stopped. We went onto the lighted stage. We could see outlines of the three judges. They asked if there was anything we needed to explain about the scene. I said no. They said, "Begin when you're ready." After a little bit of preparation, we went into the scene. In five minutes, we were finished, and we left, as another hopeful couple passed us.

The first thing I said on leaving the audition was that if they accepted us on what we did in there, I wouldn't accept. I said I was just terrible, and that I was sorry I wasn't better. My partner thought I'd lost my mind. What I was doing was simply priming myself for the eventual turn down. Two weeks later, I received a postcard from the Studio saying I was a member of the Actors Studio. I called my actress partner. She, too, had received a postcard saying the work was good but that she would have to audition again, if she were so inclined.

Lee Strasberg's distinguished Actors Studio is a very exclusive school, and to be a member in the early fifties was quite prestigious. From the day it opened its doors in 1947 to the year 1999, it admitted only nine hundred students (an average of only eighteen per year). Once accepted into membership, a person remains a member for life. The Actors Studio's own description of its purpose is "a studio; a private, protected workshop where actors, playwrights, and directors, united not by fame or success, but by talent and intention, could practice their craft, bravely, even recklessly, out of the limelight and free of the pressures of the commercial world." Its members include such giants in the field as Dustin Hoffman, Marlon Brando, Robert De Niro, Paul Newman, Carroll O'Connor, Sidney Poitier, Rod Steiger, Robin Williams, Shelley Winters, and Gene Wilder.

When one is using "The Method," he reaches into his own memories, experiences and emotions to develop a character. While other techniques deal with text and language, this system deals with psychology. It gives a character more dimensions.

Stage actor Floyd Oydegaard explains how The Method is used to prepare for a role: "Need to have some emotion for a funeral scene? Go to a funeral and watch those around you. Absorb! Need harsher realities? Find a harsh reality. It's a hard task, and many method actors find that the experience has changed them too much in some way, and they lose a purity of ignorance really soon. (That's why a technical director or expert comes in and teaches or trains most actors to be doctors. A method actor would go to an actual ER and be there with a certain doctor all week to understand it all better and to really be a part of the experience.)"

The work at the Studio was really for me the growth of a professional. Incidentally, my actress partner got into the Studio two years later. Everybody, every actor, every actress wanted to act at the Studio. Only the members could, and every member wanted to act on the Studio stage. One had to sign up weeks in advance to get on stage, and rehearsal room was at a premium. I had a fistfight for rehearsal space in the studio prop room. The actor I had the fight with is still acting. I see him occasionally on the tube. The girl I was doing the scene with was married to a successful writer who wrote for TV. She commented on the fact that there was no rehearsal space, so she said she rented a room in a hotel in Brooklyn for three weeks so we could work uninterrupted. We rehearsed during the days and, again, sex was a part of the rehearsals. I spent many nights at the hotel and waited for her to come back the next day. She had to go home at night to her husband. We rehearsed the three weeks, and the time to show it came.

This was to be my first scene at the Studio in front of the members with Lee Strasberg as the moderator/teacher. We began the scene and, halfway through, I stopped and said, "It isn't working."

I heard Lee's voice, "Continue."

I looked at him.

"Continue," he said. "Continue."

After a bit of time, I did continue and finished the scene. Strasberg explained, not kindly, that one never stops a scene, for two reasons: 1) there is a partner who is working with you, and 2) if you worked correctly, you would not be monitoring yourself. This was my intro-

duction and first personal critique from Lee at the Studio. I was to have many more. Well, not many—maybe six in all. Of course, I witnessed many scenes, too, and learned, again, by watching and listening.

I did a show early in my career, *The Male Animal*. I did it in summer stock. I suppose it's still being done in some stock company or some civic theatre somewhere in this country. There's nothing unusual about doing one of these family shows. It's good entertainment. In those days, I was—or thought I was—hot stuff as an actor. My actor's ego was unbelievable. Well, I played one of those juvenile characters (Wally Myers). The character makes about three entrances—enters and leaves—and he has about ten speaking lines. At one of the performances, I was relaxing in the green room, waiting for my cue. Well, something distracted me (probably a pretty apprentice) and, before I knew it, my cue had come and gone. I rushed from the green room bent on making my entrance, no matter the circumstances. The stage manager stopped me and explained that the actors on stage had continued with the play, and told me to pay more attention to my work. I was devastated. I waited for the second act curtain and rushed on stage, all apologetic. The actors who had been on stage had not missed me and had not realized that I had missed my entrance! The play is so constructed that the character could be cut from the play without changing the main thrust of the play. All this time, I thought I was indispensable when actually I was really unimportant to the play. It brought my ego down considerably, and was probably a good lesson.

Calder Willingham, a writer from the South, was permitted to come into the Studio as an observer. He had written the novel End As a Man about life in a southern military academy. That youngster from the "Burning Bush", the survivor from the Nazi concentration camps [twenty-three-year-old Jack Garfein], **had also gotten into the** Studio. He was quite enthused about Willingham's novel. He approached eight actors in the Studio to work on the novel as a three-act play. I was one of the actors. We all got copies of the novel, read it and agreed that it could be fashioned into a play.

End As a Man was set at the Citadel. Jocko deParis, a senior, was a Hitler-type character, powerful and cruel. He used Roger Gatt (Albert's character)—a big, not-too-bright football player—to help him haze the freshmen. DeParis knew that when Gatt was drunk, he became quite dangerous to the people around him. Such was deParis' plan of intimidation. This continued until the underclassmen finally stood up to him.

We, the actors, and the "youngster," now our director, met every afternoon for about four hours, five days a week, to hammer out a loose-structured play, with scenes that progressed to acts which continued to curtain. I say loose because we followed the book as much as we could, but we knew we would have to improvise a great deal. I had done a great deal of improvisation in the Footlight Bar, as I've related earlier. The "youngster" had been an avid observer of the Footlight Bar improvisations and had formed a way of asking questions pertinent to the character in the given circumstances of the book within the loose structure of the scene. This was an informal way of directing, and was quite effective. In all, it took us about a month to finally say that we had something we could work with to get to the final completed play.

It won't be hard for the "trivia buff" to discover the actors who appeared in the play. One name that doesn't appear is Jimmy Dean's. He rehearsed with us for three or four weeks as an underclassman with a few lines, but then dropped out. I got to know him well. I did a live TV show that he had a small part in.

The improvisations on the characters and on the given circumstances of the novel, and now the play, went very well, considering that, as a group, we had not worked closely together before. In order to cast General, Commanding Officer of the school, we went outside the Studio membership. I can't remember why we did so, but we did. The actor who played the General [Frank M. Thomas] has had a good professional career.

Before these rehearsals began, the others and I worked regularly in live TV. It was our bread and butter. If there ever was a "brat pack" in those days, it certainly was us. We turned down all work for about five months to concentrate on bringing this piece of work up to snuff. We had no grandiose ideas about the finished product. We were content to show it at the Studio to Strasberg and the members. It was truly a labor of love and the purest ensemble group I have ever been with. We all felt good about showing it at the Studio because it was a "first." To date, no one had done a production in the Studio, with Studio members, solely for the Studio. We were trailblazers.

The day came for the showing of our endeavors. The members, of course, came, but also a few invited guests—as many as seating allowed. We did the play with minimal set, props, lighting, and no costumes, except that we all wore similar tank tops. We went through the play and finished, and Lee treated it like a class. There was a critique from Lee and the members. On the whole, we were applauded for the good work and dedication. I know Lee was very pleased and touched that we made the sacrifices to do the kind of work that he was teaching.

After the showing and the critique, we all left and thought no more about what we had done. I know that I considered it nothing more than a class exercise.

The "youngster" had other ideas that we discovered later. One of the invited guests was a young, wealthy woman [Claire Heller] who became enthralled with the play and what we had accomplished with it. She told us she wanted to produce this play with these actors off-Broadway. In those days, a show could be mounted off-Broadway for less than $15,000. Today [1990], it will take a quarter to half a million. In fact, a few years later, I produced and starred in a play I liked Off-Broadway for $12,000.

We all agreed to do it. It meant a few more weeks of rehearsal until a theatre was hired, the sets built, costumes made, props and lighting obtained, etc. The billing was to be alphabetical. All this was accomplished and we opened [at the Theatre De Lys in the Village] for a limited run, meaning if we flop, we close, but not immediately. We had enough money for a two-week run.

All this was academic because we opened and we were a "hit." All the reviews were good. Beyond good. They were great! The Billboard called it "End As a Man, an Actors Studio Production." This was just like "The Three Sisters, a Moscow Art Theatre Production". I mean we were heroes of dedicated theatre.

Pat Hingle, who played deParis' roommate Harry Koble, recalls opening night and the cast party afterward. Ida Salmi had come to see her son perform. "She was more comfortable speaking her own language than English," Hingle says. "She seemed to feel out of place there." She appeared to him to be a strong, stoic woman, not given to open displays of pride. "Like a pioneer woman," he said. Her devotion to her son was evident, though, by the fact that she was right there by his side that night to lend her support.

We ran downtown for four months to full houses, SRO (standing room only).

On September 16th, the *New York Herald Tribune's* theater reporter, Walter F. Kerr, described Salmi's scene in the second act as "an immensely funny but dramatically unprogressive interlude with a magnificently lame-brained football player."

William Hawkins reported in the *New York World-Telegram* and *The Sun*, "As the simple-minded football player, Albert Salmi has a lengthy drunk scene and fight which is an extraordinary *tour de force*. As a hot-tempered monster, he achieves a merciless physical degradation."

After about three months our female producer said she made enough profit to move us to another theatre—on Broadway. She wanted to make our modest offering a Broadway show! The cost for this project was about $75,000. How much today? Oh, about five million. We all felt quite honored. None of us had been on Broadway before.

"*End As a Man*", says Pat Hingle, "was the first play to go from Off-Broadway to Broadway. Others have done it since then, but this was the first."

We knew we had a good show. The reviews and the full houses proved it, and we were learning with every performance more and more about our characters.

The plan was to stay where we were...until a Broadway house was hired, a new set built, new everything, including marvelous costumes. The amazing thing is that from our first gathering at the Studio to our opening on Broadway, all the pieces seemed to fall into

place. There were small problems not worthy of mention. It all was just unbelievably smooth.

To Salmi, though, there was now a "fly in the ointment." The hype on the promotional items was distasteful to him, and the play was becoming too commercialized for this idealistic young man. Jack Garfein said they had to plead with Albert to keep him in the show.

We opened on Broadway [at the Vanderbilt Theatre]. **This is where naiveté and inexperience comes in. The learning procession continues. It was re-reviewed as a Broadway play and the reviews were lukewarm. What is praised off-Broadway is examined with tougher expectations on Broadway.**

Journal American reporter John McClain came to their Broadway opening night, then wrote, "...somebody has done a lot of rewriting since I first saw it [Off-Broadway] and I'm afraid the result has weakened rather than strengthened the basic structure."

Nevertheless, the critics still seemed to like Albert. Wrote John Chapman of the *New York Daily News*, "There are a number of lively scenes, the best of them being a drinking and gambling bout in which Salmi plays the stupid victim."

According to the playbill on November 30, 1953, the general was no longer being played by Frank M. Thomas. In the cast now were Ben Gazzara, William Smithers, Arthur Storch, Albert Salmi, R. G. Armstrong, Paul Richards, Pat Hingle, and Mark Richman.

Armstrong recalls how he and Albert were very much alike in those days. "We lived our parts. We felt swept along."

The lukewarm reviews, the large Broadway house we could not half fill, the small (sometimes nonexistent) salaries that we got for over half a year, were taking their toll. Actors were leaving to go to work on TV for money. The replacements never had the spark of the original and, in about three weeks, we closed. The great experiment ended.

This play was later made into the 1957 film *The Strange One*. Pat Hingle reprised his role for the movie, but Albert wouldn't. "At that time," says Hingle, "Albert was a big, tow-headed guy with a boyish face. They

Good friend Rod Steiger visits Albert and Claire. *(Claire Kirby Hooton)*

kept putting him in dumb roles, and he wanted to get away from that." Hingle feels that for Albert to have portrayed Roger Gatt in the film "would have given him power." His career could have really taken off, he believes. "No one could play that role like Albert could."

Hingle wasn't the only person disappointed by Salmi's decision. "To me, one of the tragedies of Albert was Lee Strasberg's overly strong influence on him early on, and Albert sort of idolized him in a very simple, sweet way. I felt that Strasberg's attitude, for me, was horrible," says Jack Garfein, who also directed the movie. Echoing Strasberg's philosophy, "Movies are not art" was Salmi's stubborn response. Garfein told him, "Albert, you created this part. It's just really wonderful and it's important. It's an ensemble work. You should be a part of it," but Albert was uncompromising. "He swallowed that false idolatry" of the stage, says Garfein.

Then Albert Salmi fell in love.

I was dating a beautiful girl at this period. She was an actress and a member of the Studio. We were getting quite serious about marriage. Her name is Claire.

After Claire Kirby had been rehearsing a scene with Jimmy Dean at the Actors Studio Albert asked if he may walk her home, and they went from the Studio far west, on 49th Street, to her apartment at the other end of town on East 66th Street. Once they got into the lobby of the stone building, he squared himself in front of her and said, "I want you to be my girl." This simply floored her. "Blew me away!" she says; and she found herself agreeing, out of sheer amazement, that she would be his girl.

"She was like a princess to Albert," recalls R. G. Amstrong. She had a tremendous respect for Albert's talent. To illustrate his ingenuity, she tells of a time in which she was doing a scene at the Actors Studio from a very sophisticated British comedy, which he was directing. Claire was to make an entrance, but Albert had intentionally locked the door. She became extremely frustrated, which provided the spark that that scene needed. "I did the scene great!" The audience loved the outcome.

"He was a very intuitive actor," says Claire. "He was an enigma. He was very bright." He was also gentle. He took good care of her and was sensitive of her feelings. What troubled Claire, though, was his reticence. Even though he could express emotion freely

Deep-sea fishing with Claire, who took this picture. *(Salmi family collection)*

onstage, he had a difficult time doing that in real life. The result was often pervasive silence. There is no word in the Finnish language that means "small talk." Salmi was comfortable with silence, but Claire wasn't. In spite of all the time they spent together, she felt that she never really knew him.

R. G. Armstrong describes it as "straight jacketing" his emotions in real life, then letting it all out on stage. "That," he says, "is what makes a great actor."

Armstrong recalls the time that Albert was doing the "to be or not to be" scene in *Hamlet*, gesturing quite dramatically, when the class burst out laughing. This was very unexpected and quite distressing. What was he doing wrong? His classmates just couldn't help it. They were seeing the boyish-looking actor, not the character. That, Salmi knew, would never do.

Salmi appeared on Broadway again in *The Rainmaker*, which opened on October 28, 1954, at the Cort Theatre. He was again playing a young, not-very-bright character, Jim Curry. In the January, 1955, issue of *Theatre Arts*

The Rainmaker on Broadway, with Darren McGavin (standing). 1954. *(Photofest)*

magazine, Maurice Zolotow said that all members of the company were "beyond reproach." The ones singled out as especially noteworthy were Geraldine Page, Cameron Prud'homme, Darren McGavin, and Albert Salmi.

Saul Colin, in the English magazine *Plays and Players*, wrote, "the real find of the evening is Albert Salmi, another alumnus of the Dramatic Workshop, who plays the young and simple-minded brother of Lizzie with rare insight and good taste. He is a remarkable actor…"

Recognition was coming at Albert now from all directions. *The New York Times* ran a large article in their drama section about him. But he felt that his youthful appearance was limiting his roles. To compensate, he wore a cap similar to his father's and smoked a cigar. He told *Times* reporter Gilbert Millstein, "I'm an actor because I want to teach someone to be better than they are," Albert said. "If an actor does a role honestly and says to an audience, 'This happens, you can rest assured of it,' maybe five, maybe ten, maybe just one will leave the theatre better than when he came in."

The Rainmaker had a fifteen-week run, then went on national tour, but Salmi stayed in New York to see what other opportunities awaited him there.

A few weeks after *The Rainmaker*, I received a telephone call from my agent, and she informed me that *Bus Stop* was in trouble out of town, and the producer was seeking a replacement. A reading was arranged in one of the theaters that was dark. By "dark," I mean that the Broadway theatre in question had no show in it at that time. I went to the theatre at the appointed time with my agent and her husband, a nappy little guy who had been a song and dance performer in vaudeville. His words I remember clearly: "Let out all stops and knock 'em in the aisles," he said.

I was loose. I had just come off a Broadway show. I had money and great expectations of a blossoming career. So I was thinking as I went in that if I blow it, that's okay.

I was called out onto the stage, the only lighting was the bare work light that is always present on stages when a show wasn't on and an audience in place. That work light was like home to me. I always like to walk around a stage with that warm stage light illuminating center stage and going to muted darkness around you. There were two chairs near the light, and the secretary to the producer was on stage. She held a script of Bus Stop and handed me a script of the show before I sat down on the folding chair. (It's always a folding chair.) I was introduced to the producer, the writer and the stage manager. They would be the ones to make the decision as to whether I got the part or not. Mind you, I hadn't seen the script before this meeting. The secretary read all the other parts and I read "Bo," the cowboy character in the play. The secretary apparently had not read the script, either. Her plodding, slow reading of the script allowed me to read ahead silently to some degree, and my enthusiastic reading was in direct contrast to her monotone reading. I'm convinced that this condition swung the balance scales in my direction. The reading took a couple hours, but it seemed a very short time to me, and we finished.

My agent, her husband, and I left the theatre, and when we were outside, my agent asked me why I hadn't come to the reading dressed in Levis and boots and a plaid shirt. I didn't have an answer. I think I didn't dress as a cowboy because I felt that the producer and writer (I had expected that they would be at the reading) had been seeing the actor I was to replace in western clothes. I didn't want them to couple me with that actor in any way. If I had picked the same costume, I was concerned they would see that actor, and it would have a negative input.

That night, I went out with some actor cronies to Sardi's bar and we lifted a few. My friends in those days have become legendary in the acting profession. I'm sure that, in some instances, I'll treat them rudely in this narrative; but on the whole, I am very fond of them, and consider it an honor to have known them.

One of those friends was actress Patricia Neal. "I first knew Albert Salmi at the Actors Studio," she says. "He was going with a friend of mine [Claire]. I got to know him then. I was very pregnant with my first daughter, and Albert's girlfriend stayed with me when my husband, Roald Dahl, was on the road with his only play, *The Honeys*. We saw that Roald liked Albert, as did I. We thought he was a divine man." Salmi and Neal had worked together earlier at the Theatre de Lys in *The Scarecrow*.

The next day after the reading, I was told the role was mine. I didn't feel tremendously happy, nor was I sad.

"We had first done the play in Philadelphia," producer Robert Whitehead told the *New York Times*. "Kim Stanley was very, very gifted, but the leading man (Cliff Robertson) wasn't right—he was physically effective, good at flinging stools around, but Bo has to have a complete innocence mixed with something dangerous, a kind of unbridled lust for life. He's not housebroken.

"Albert Salmi had just closed in *The Rainmaker* and I grabbed him. He suddenly brought Kim to life, and she knew it, knew the play hadn't been working, that it didn't have its life force until the two of them were together. I remember the enormous sense of relief when I felt we'd achieved the inside of the play."

I knew that the next month or so would entail a great deal of work and dedication. Time was of the essence. I flew up to Philadelphia immediately. Every spare minute, I read the play and re-read the play. I never imagined how the other characters in the play looked, sounded, or acted. I knew that soon enough I would know. When I got to Philadelphia, I was told the company was at a particular hotel, so I registered in another hotel for two reasons. The first was that I had no desire to accidentally run into the actor I was replacing and, two, I was aware that the actors knew their roles, so they didn't have

any studying to do, so they would be socializing and having some drinks. I could not take the luxury of relaxing and socializing. I had work to do. I asked for and got a girl to "cue" me on the script. She and I would go over and over the script to the wee morning hours. She was a very pretty girl, sister to the producer's secretary. I never once made a pass at her—the concentrated work was that intense—though she does come back into my life some years later.

I arrived in Philly on a Monday, and saw the play performed Tuesday night. The actor was not strong in the role. His background had not been the stage but, rather, Hollywood. The trap of the Hollywood actor was to be ingratiating. The role demanded the opposite—that is, until the third act—but to play the roughness to the gentleness had to be orchestrated with great care.

Salmi's character, Bo Decker, grows tremendously, beginning in Act One as the boisterous, headstrong, naive young cowboy, then becoming the more sensitive, gentle lover at the end of Act Three, in his determination to win the hand of beautiful Cherie.

My first rehearsal was called for Wednesday afternoon, after the matinee performance. I took a very roundabout way to the theatre. I still didn't want to meet the actor I was replacing; in fact, I never had met him. It would have been embarrassing for both of us.

I went backstage and onto the stage. The Bus Stop cafe set was there, the folding chairs set in a semi-circle were there, and the ever-present work light was there. The difference was the house lights were on, and I saw the solitary figure in the audience. I introduced myself to this solitary man, the director of the play. He said he was happy to have me join the company. The cast took a while to join me on the stage. They had just performed the show, and had taken time to get their make-up off, have a quick bite, and come to rehearsal. There were the folding chairs for each of us, and we sat in no particular order.

This was to be a sitting reading, just to get the feeling of where people were coming from. We began at a couple pages before the entrance of my character. I was nervous. I hadn't memorized my role completely, though I was well up in it, thanks to the pretty little girl who was "cueing" me. I took my cue and began to read.

The Broadway star.

I got no further than the first two lines, when the director stopped me and gave me line readings. In other words, he told me how to say the lines and what inflections to use. I waited until he was finished and began again, from the point of interruption. He stopped me again and again, and went through the process of line reading.

My mind was racing at this point, and I considered three salient points: I was rushed up to Philly, the director had seen the reading in New York, and there was no one else on the horizon for this role. I had him by the short hairs, but how to be forceful without alienating everyone in the theatre?

I closed the script. I can't imagine what everyone was thinking when I closed the script, but I've got a pretty good idea. The show was going to close if I didn't work out, and indications were I wasn't going to work out. I waited for what seemed hours; actually it probably was some twenty seconds. No one said anything. We all just sat. Finally, I spoke, "Mr. Director (I used his name), I was in the audience last night, and the actor playing this part was giving you your line readings, and you're firing him! We don't have a lot of time, so please leave me to my own devices."

To his credit, he never again gave me another line reading, except for the curtain line for either the first or second act—I can't remember which one. He asked that I give him the line reading for curtain. Opening nights in Philly and New York, I didn't use his line reading, but, thereafter, when I knew he was in the audience, I would do it his way and invariably, he would come backstage and say I gave a good performance that particular night.

The company continued performing in Philly with the other actor. During the day I would rehearse with the company, and every night the "cueing" continued.

Jack Garfein tells us about one of the rehearsals. ""What happened was that it's a scene where Cherie comes running into the bus stop, and Albert comes running after her. [Director] Clurman said, 'Great, wonderful. Kim, wonderful. Albert, wonderful. And now we'll take a lunch break.' And as we took a lunch break, Albert walked over to Harold and said, 'Listen, Harold, I'm not an actor that likes to be flattered. I like people to be direct with me, and you said to Kim that she was brilliant. Absolutely! I kept looking. I saw that woman was cold to her toes, and when she went up to the stove, I saw the heat moving through her body. It was extraordinary. Me, I felt nothing. There was no heat at all. I had no sensation of that sort. And you said 'excellent' to her and 'excellent' to me.' Harold said to him, 'Albert, Cherie is cold. You are *hot*, even though it's winter, because you're chasing and running after her.'"

One night late, there was a knock at my door. The pretty girl, who faithfully was "cueing" me, had left a few hours earlier. When I opened the door, there was the leading lady from the play, with a bottle and a couple glasses. She told me she had left the hotel she was in and registered into my hotel. She was in a robe, and said she liked what I was doing in the role, and said she was very lonely. This, as you can understand, was a dilemma for me. I was very attracted to this lovely actress, and I knew the professional dance that actors and actresses perform.

The condition is simple in that if one is doing a love story in the theatre, in films or television, the time element to get to know one another is telescoped and the two fictional lovers must become, in reality, lovers. Once this dance is completed, the love and familiarity the audience sees on stage—or in the movies or on TV, to a large degree—is real. The closeness on stage is something that one does not have to act, because the actors have already been to bed.

This was my predicament in the late hours of this particular night. I told this lovely actress that I was exhausted from trying to memorize the role (no, I didn't say I had a headache), and that I needed to rest, if ever I was going to get up in the part. At this point, it was better to get up in the role, rather than to get up in bed! I told her I was very tempted. I was, but it would have to wait. She took it in stride, said goodnight, and left.

About an hour later, there came, again, a knock on the door. The knock awoke me from a sound sleep, but instantly I was ready and randy—amazing what a few minutes of sleep will accomplish! I didn't put anything on and went to the door. I opened the door. Imagine my surprise to see my leading lady's husband standing there! Imagine his surprise to see me, naked, answering the door. Once we got over the initial surprise, he asked me if his wife was in my room. He told me he'd discovered that she had changed hotels. I told him that she wasn't in my room and that I didn't know where she was, that it was late, and I was tired, and good night. I closed the door and breathed a sigh of relief.

The rehearsals continued. The lady never brought the subject up again. The work was hard but within a week, I was ready to go on. The tenth day after my arrival in Philly, I went onstage as Bo Decker in Bus Stop. The performance went well.

In September, 1955, *Plays and Players* reported, "Albert Salmi—who had only a few days of rehearsal—emerges as a growing actor destined for stardom."

The producer was in the audience. After the show, he came backstage to my dressing room and asked how I felt about opening in New York the end of next week. I said to him that I was still rough in the role but that I felt I could smooth out the rough spots for an opening next week in New York. I said I'd be willing and, if he was comfortable with me, let's do it. That producer was and is one of the most intelligent, talented and decisive men I've ever known. He said, "We're on," and we did open the following week. Before he left my dressing room that evening, he asked me if I would be interested in investing in Bus Stop; if so, he could work out the details. I respectfully declined, for somewhere inside me I had an uneasy feeling about Bus Stop succeeding. To this day, I regret not investing. The royalties from the play and the sale to the movies would have made me comfortably wealthy.

During one performance in Philly, Bo orders a meal and then sits down to eat. The actress playing the waitress put the meal on the counter and a bottle of milk, but she forgot the glass. I picked up the bottle of milk and started to drink it. As I was drinking from the bottle, I wondered how much of it I could drink. I just kept that bottle tipped up and kept drinking. I sensed a muffled gasp from the audience, and an approval, little hand claps, little laughter. They liked my drinking the milk. I kept drinking until I finished all the milk. The house exploded, the applause stopped the show. Needless to say, at every performance after that one, I drank a bottle of milk; and the applause stopped the show at every subsequent performance. The actor learns from the audience, if the actor is aware. The audience actually cued me in to drinking all the milk.

When I arrived in Philly, and through the rehearsal and the playing, the understudy for Bo was after me all the time. He wanted to play the role—it was his role, he should have gotten it when they let the other actor go, he knew more about the character than I did, he was physically closer to Bo than I was—he went on and on, day in and day out. He was getting to be a pest, and I knew he would never stop. I was determined to put an end to his constant asking.

The company moved to New York, and we opened in a beautiful small theatre just off Eighth Avenue.

Produced by Robert Whitehead and Roger L. Stevens, *Bus Stop* was first presented on March 2, 1955, at The Music Box theatre in New York City. Starring with Salmi were Phyllis Love, Elaine Stritch, Lou Polan, Kim Stanley, Anthony Ross, Patrick McVey, and Crahan Denton.

The reviews were great. After opening night, the cast of the opening play, traditionally, would go to Sardi's, and about one o'clock they would get tear sheets of all the reviews to be published in the next day's papers. I don't know who went to Sardi's. I didn't. Why? I didn't have to read the reviews. I knew by the audience reaction that we were a hit. There wasn't a question in my mind. I just walked up Broadway to Central Park; I walked for a while in the park and took a cab home. It wasn't until the following day that I read the reviews. They were very, very good. I went by the theatre that afternoon, and there was a long line of ticket buyers.

Bus Stop was voted the best of the 1954-55 season on Broadway by the critics of national magazines and New York newspapers.

The cast became overnight celebrities, and everyone in New York wanted an interview. I gave as many interviews as asked for. If someone had questions, I would answer them.

One interview I gave, I regretted. I told the interviewer that *Bus Stop* was really a piece-of-fluff play, a boy-meets-girl play, nothing more, nothing less. It was not and could not be considered a "classic" in any sense of the word. I believed what I said. I shouldn't have said it. It hurt the writer, Bill Inge. He didn't talk to me for a long, long time. I didn't blame him. He was a very sensitive, shy man and I hurt him unnecessarily.

The play had been running about two, three weeks when I told my understudy that he would get his chance to play the role on the following Wednesday evening performance. I told him not to tell anyone, but I would not come to the theatre for that evening performance. I had been invited after Wednesday matinee to have dinner at Stark Young's. Stark Young was retired, but he was considered the greatest New York reviewer of drama that ever lived. His pen was the most powerful weather vane in New York theatre when he was active. He knew no peer.

The Wednesday matinee came. My understudy was very, very nervous, and I swear all the blood had gone out of his face. I said "Good luck" to him and went to Stark Young's for dinner.

Stark Young's life was theatre. He lived it, talked about it, breathed it. It took up his whole life, even in retirement. The meal was good, and his talk at the dinner table was inspiring. It was getting close for me to leave for the theatre for the evening performance, but I made no move to the door. The later it got, the more agitated Stark Young became. He finally started pushing me out the door. He realized I wasn't going to make the curtain. I then told him the tale of the badgering understudy, and that that same understudy is just about to go onstage. I expected Young to get angry at the way I treated the play and paying audience, for he was a pure theatre person. When he heard the story, he laughed and said that I had administered the perfect medicine. He also said that all the theatrical community would also know what I did, because the understudy would tell his agent, he would tell his friends, he would tell ev-

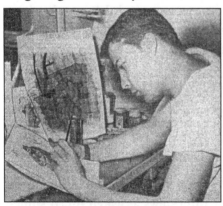

Awaiting his cue.
(The New York Journal-American)

Furniture shopping at Hammacher Schlemmer.

eryone and anyone that he was going to play Bo. The problem with that was that the theatre was sold out, and not many of the people got to see him.

The next evening, when I went to the theatre, I made my excuses, telling them I had been under the weather and just couldn't get to the theatre the night before. I saw the understudy and asked him how it went. He said, "Fine." The cast members said otherwise. The upshot of the whole thing was that the understudy never asked me again to let him play the part. Sometimes people think they can do something when, in fact, they cannot.

When not on stage, Salmi enjoyed fencing whenever he could engage anyone in a match, and would sometimes create paintings of his character.

He knew they had really made it once a major magazine covered the play. "I was walking along Broadway shortly after *Bus Stop* had opened and I heard a shout," says Robert Sugarman, Actors Studio stage manager and friend of Salmi's. "It was Al bouncing down the sidewalk, waving a copy of *Life* that had a big spread on the play. That has always been my image—joy and success. He was so thrilled."

The March 28, 1955 issue of *Life* contained a four-page article entitled "Best Comedy of the Season." He and Kim Stanley were highly praised and, out of the seven accompanying photos, Salmi was in four of them.

There was a fundraiser held very shortly after this for CARE by the American National Theatre and Academy (ANTA). Stars of current Broadway hits were asked to recreate a scene from their plays for this special, which would be telecast via closed-circuit to movie theaters throughout the U.S. on the evening of Monday, March 28, 1955. Salmi was among them, as was David Burns, who played straight man to a child in his segment. Salmi had been quite fond of David ever since his ushering days at the Alvin theatre. The video, possibly the only one in existence of this ANTA fundraiser, is available for viewing at the UCLA Film and Television Archives. Spotlighted in the *Bus Stop* segment was Albert's blustery entrance scene. Unfortunately, the "snack," in which he drinks an entire quart of milk at once, was among those cut from the scene for this occasion.

Now that he was earning good money, Albert got an apartment of his own. Albert asked Claire to come live with him.

On April 29, 1955, Salmi received the first of many awards and honors. During the Page One Ball held at the Hotel Sheraton-Astor, the Newspaper Guild of New York presented to him their Page One Award (now called the Tony) in Theatre for persuasive acting in *The Rainmaker* and *Bus Stop*, the other recipient being his favorite co-star, Kim Stanley. They were considered by these seasoned journalists to be the crème de la crème of the theatre world. Winning the Page One Award in Science that year was the nation's hero, Dr. Jonas E. Salk, and the Page One Award in Sports went to Dr. Roger Bannister for being the first to break the four-minute-mile record.

Also, Salmi and his leading lady appeared on the cover of the prestigious *Theatre Arts* magazine in June, 1955. Inside was an article about three of the principals of this play, one of which was Albert. In the previous month's issue reviewer Maurice Zolotow wrote, "...and Salmi, a man of prodigious energy, a magnificent voice and complete stage presence, must also be careful that he does not fall into the noble savage rut."

We hadn't been running very long when the producer told me he was getting up a national company of Bus Stop. I told him I would like to take it out on the road. I knew it would be a first-class tour

Bus Stop

and I wanted to see the country. It's unheard of for the star of a play running in New York to leave the play and go on tour. I'm probably the only actor ever to have done it. My one stipulation was that my girlfriend Claire be hired as "general understudy," meaning she would cover the three female characters in the play. This was agreed to by

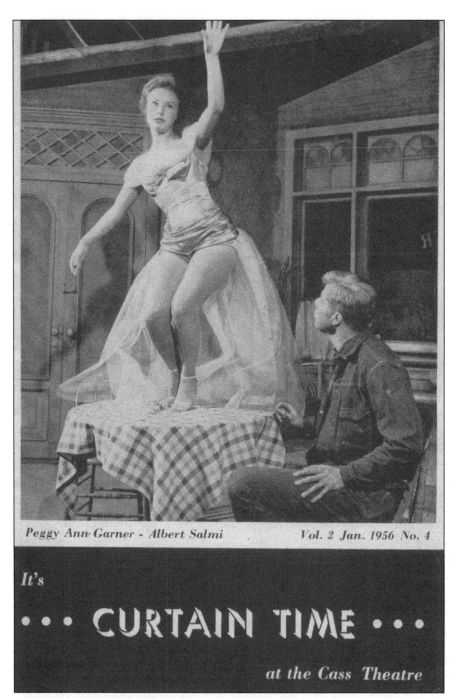

Peggy Ann Garner - Albert Salmi   Vol. 2 Jan. 1956 No. 4

It's

··· CURTAIN TIME ···

at the Cass Theatre

The *Bus Stop* national tour, with Peggy Ann Garner.

everyone except Claire. She didn't want the tour; she preferred to remain in New York. I was disheartened, but I understood. She probably would never get a chance to play and, if she did, it would be difficult for her because she had to memorize all three parts. She would not have gotten enough rehearsal to feel comfortable.

That's true, of course, but Claire says it's not the reason she turned it down. Rather, it was because she knew she would feel pressured to marry Albert if she went with them on this tour. "I was scared of the commitment," she said. She feels that staying in New York had been the right decision for her.

We got the new cast. Peggy Ann Garner was to be my leading lady. Peggy Ann was a Hollywood actress, former child star whose knowledge of theatre was limited. Peggy Ann was not particularly good in the role, but she was enthusiastic.

She was a petite, blonde lady originally from Ohio; and many have commented on her perky enthusiasm and bubbly personality. Twenty-three years old, Peggy Ann was four years younger than Albert, but she had been in show business much longer. Her mother, Virginia, had arranged appearances for her in summer stock and modeling jobs when Peggy Ann was only five. Mother and daughter then moved to Hollywood and the very assertive Virginia got her into films. Garner's acting talent won her a special Academy Award as "outstanding child performer of 1945" for her unforgettable work in *A Tree Grows in Brooklyn* when she was only thirteen.

Garner had appeared in eighteen films from 1938 through 1949, but as she grew up, her film career started to wane. Not ready to give up the career she loved, Peggy Ann then turned to the stage. She had wanted so badly to play Cherie on Broadway, and was acutely disappointed when Kim Stanley got the part.

Peggy Ann had been married once, to actor/singer Richard Hayes, with whom she had starred in the television series *Two Girls Named Smith*. Less than three years later, Hayes had obtained a divorce in Juarez, Mexico. Despite that, she told reporters that what she wanted most was marriage and a house full of children.

In a later *Modern Screen* interview, Garner described her feelings about working with Albert on the *Bus Stop* tour: "Albert had been in the New York company; he was from the Actors' Studio, which at that time was at

Peggy Ann Garner.

the height of its fame. He was the toast of Broadway and was being hailed as the new Marlon Brando. When I heard he was to be my co-star, I was scared to death." Her interviewer, added, "However, he was gallant and courteous and she soon learned she had nothing to fear from him. They toured the country with the national company for almost a year."

Our first stop was Colorado, and we traveled by train. A national company travels by train. Touring companies tour in buses. Central City has a big Summer Arts Festival, and we were to be its centerpiece, appearing in the famous Opera House.

In the souvenir booklet of Central City's 1955 festival season, writer Ward Morehouse states, "During the bleak months of winter, the population hovers around 400, but during the summertime Festival, old Central bulges, churns and pulses with people, its streets packed with cars bearing the license plates of all 48 states. More than 500,000 visitors arrived in 1954."

Elsewhere in the booklet is a section that deals with this play: "In keeping with the Central City tradition of presenting 'only the finest in dramatic and musical presentations,' the stage of the famous Opera House is occupied during the 1955 August play season by still another prize winner. *Bus Stop*, termed by *Life* magazine as 'the best comedy of the season,' reviewed by *Time* magazine as 'the finest play of the season,' and winner of *Variety*'s Poll as 'the best show and best acting of the year,' is presented to Central City audiences for three weeks starting August 6.

"Supporting Peggy Ann Garner is Albert Salmi, re-creating his original Broadway role of Cowboy Bo Decker. According to *Life* magazine: 'As blustering Bo, Albert Salmi creates a comic masterpiece.' With this impression

Peggy Ann Garner and Albert Salmi in the national tour of *Bus Stop*, 1955. *(Photofest)*

echoed by the New York critics, Opera House audiences have a rare treat in store as Albert Salmi, sensation of the current New York theatre scene, re-creates his famous role in the Central City production of *Bus Stop*."

With that kind of advance notice, I could not get a bad review on the road. They were preconditioned to accept my performance. I could walk through the performance and be considered "marvelous." I tried hard to keep the performance up, but it's always party time on the

road; and in Central City, I bedded Peggy Ann—or did she bed me?

Central City is about four blocks long with thirty saloons. The original "face on the barroom floor" can be found in this quaint town. One night we partied very heavily and come morning, with very little sleep and a wall-banging hangover, I was ill prepared to do the matinee. At this particular night's festivities was a wealthy uranium miner. In the morning, over breakfast, he saw my distress. He said he was going to help me. I said okay, and we took off in his truck. After some driving and bumping and inhaling dirt and dust, which compounded my hangover, we got to one of his uranium mines. He took me to a large bucket, large enough for two men to stand in. He asked me to get into the bucket. I realized he was going to lower me into the mine. The bucket's clearance down the shaft was only a few inches, so he warned me to keep my elbows in the bucket. He said that when the bucket got to the bottom, I was to get out and walk around for five or ten minutes. I followed orders: I kept my elbows in, I took my walk on the bottom, I signaled that I was ready to come up. When I got to the top and climbed out of the bucket, I found my hangover gone and I felt wonderful. He explained that the only air down at the bottom was pure oxygen, and that's what I'd been breathing when I was down there. These days, you'll see professional athletes using oxygen. Its recuperative properties are amazing.

Here's one last story about Central City while we were playing there. There was the great two-horse race, "Nashua" vs. "Swaps." National Interest, it was a horse race to bet. Why not? You had a fifty-fifty chance. Swaps was the horse from the west [having won the Kentucky Derby earlier that year], and Nashua was the horse from the east. East is east and west is west, but these horses were going to meet. Since I was in the West, I bet everything I had and the following week's salary on Swaps with a local bookie. Do I have to tell you? Swaps lost, Nashua took me to the cleaners. Some years later, I did a movie in Kentucky [*The Flim-Flam Man*, filmed in Lexington] and I was told that Nashua was at stud on one of the Bluegrass farms. I think it was Spindletop. At any rate, I went out to Spindletop to see this horse. We were taken to a white-fenced field, and there in the far end of the field, lying down, chewing his cud or whatever horses chew, was Nashua. When he saw us, he got up and trotted directly to us as if greeting old friends. When he got to the fence, I swear he looked directly at me and smiled. I raised my arm to hit him when, quick like a rabbit, he grabbed my forearm in his mouth and held tight. I wrestled my arm free and looked at my sleeve. It was ruined with saliva and cud and crud. It occurred to me then and there that this horse took me to the cleaners twice in his life. It's a small world, after all.

One more story—this one about the people in Colorado. There was a great deal of old wealth in Denver; probably still is. The company was invited to an afternoon brunch/cocktail lawn party. We all went. As the afternoon progressed, the actor who was playing the bus driver had a little too much to drink and, coupled with the heat of the day, he became ill. I took him and led him to the house so he could lie down, out of the sun. As we were walking toward the house, our gracious hostess stopped us and said she didn't want an actor to get sick all over her house. She suggested that he would be comfortable in one of the cars in the driveway. I thought about the incident for days after. In some arenas, actors are still considered unsavory characters. I thought to myself that the hostess' ancestors, the builders of the fortune, were probably great people and were like a clear mountain stream. The hostess, however, was the residue of this clear mountain stream. She was the muddy pond at the bottom.

The company left for Los Angeles and I, for one, was happy to go. When we got to L.A., we discovered that our director had flown out from New York to take out of the play all the "improvements" that the actors had put in. It's a good policy, because some of the unconscious "improvements" really aren't improvements, but only tend to distract from the play's original intent. We had a few days of cleaning, sharpening and tightening the play, and then the director asked me if I'd like to go see Clifford Odets. I knew Clifford from the Studio. He was a constant visitor and I'd had lunch with him a number of times. I looked forward to seeing him. The director and I (oh what the hell, the director was Harold Clurman) went to Clifford's hotel, located on the Sunset Strip. When we got to his apartment, Clifford let us in and we exchanged warm greetings. Drinks were served and we sat down to talk. There was a fourth person in the living room, a surly, rude, uncommunicative Marlon Brando. I'd never met him before, and this meeting was not auspicious. I doubt he said more than ten words and constantly stared into space. I made no effort to converse with Marlon. It seemed pointless. So I turned my attention to Clifford, who was a little uneasy about Marlon. Clifford had come out to California to write a Biblical film. I knew that he was doing it, so in the course of conversation, I asked him how the screenplay was coming. His answer to my question was, "I'm sorry, Albert, but there's no role in it for you." I don't know what happens to people. He didn't answer my question. He, rather, assumed that I was asking for a job. I told him that he had misunderstood my question as I was committed to the play for the year and could not accept a job, even if offered. I made my excuses and left. That was the last time I saw Clifford.

The company rehearsed a few more days and we opened in L.A. [at the Huntington Hartford theatre in Hollywood] **to rave reviews. The fawning Hollywood community rushed in with their praises and invitations, the audiences were receptive, and I met a lot of actors, directors, and producers. One never knew what those people were thinking, and the conversation was so shallow that I wanted out of L.A. The theatre had brainwashed me about Hollywood. I had an instant dislike. I've flown in and out of L.A. many times to do guest-starring roles on most of the TV series that were in production—mostly westerns, but others also; but I just flew in and flew out. This play forced me to be in L.A. for a much longer time. A stifling experience. I wasn't ready for it. The show ran uneventfully in L.A. I made acquaintances, but no friends. The evenings were never free because we had a show to do. In those days, most New York actors were still in New York and had not made the exodus. That came later. So my New York actor friends were three thousand miles away.**

Salmi's friend, R. G. Amstrong, later said that he and Albert had both felt out of place, even awkward, in California. The New York stage was where their hearts were.

Actually, Salmi was the only actor in this troupe to whom Los Angeles critic, Clayton Cole, was even halfway kind. Of Salmi, he wrote, "His work is the one interesting thing in the production," but felt that, even so, Albert couldn't carry the play alone.

We closed the limited run in Los Angeles and moved up to [the Geary theatre in] **San Francisco. The play was on a schedule. We had to be at a certain place at a certain date. Eight weeks was our longest stay in the large cities. Three nights was the shortest stay in smaller**

cities. On the road, you drink and eat and do the show, you party occasionally, sightsee. Mostly, it's the work. Eight performances a week and living out of a suitcase.

Reviewer Hortense Morton noted, "Although a smash hit in New York, William Inge's fine play, like some excellent vintage wines, does not travel well due to careless direction and miscasting."

The producer flew out to San Francisco to see the show, visit San Francisco, and, because he knew I loved to fish, he wanted to take me fishing. True to his word, he chartered a fishing boat. Poles, reels, and bait were provided. All we had to do was show up at Fisherman's Wharf. Our stage manager, young Mike Chase, was invited to join us. (Mike's mother was Mary C. Chase. She wrote the play Harvey. I did the play with the Stanley Woolf players in the Catskills for ten weeks, years before. It's really a funny play and still an enjoyed play in many summer stock theatres.) Off we went, the three of us. The water was a little choppy, and I could see Mike was not a sailor. When we put out our lines, Mike disappeared up forward. The producer and I actively fished. Mike's pole was unattended in its holder. It became apparent that Mike's line had something on it. We called him aft to tend to his pole. He started to reel it in and, after a while, the hook came up. It was hooked onto a dead seagull. Mike lost it. He started throwing up all over the boat, and he couldn't stop. He was sick! Later, he said his mother had told him not to embarrass himself on the boat. So he hid up forward because he wasn't feeling well, but then when he saw that seagull, he couldn't help himself. Poor kid! We tried to make him feel better about the event. He was ashamed over something he had no control over.

One afternoon, after a matinee, I lay down in my dressing room for a nap. I wasn't asleep long when there was a big bang. I was sure a truck had smashed into the building. I went outside to see just what it was that hit the building, and there was nothing. I found out later that I had experienced my first earthquake. (In 1971, I went through another one in L.A. There were deaths, freeway collapsing, and I received a broken rib from it.)

As I remember, the next stop was Detroit [the Cass Theatre], a forgettable city except for one thing. The biography in the playbill mentioned the fact that I had studied fencing. This was quite true. I had studied diligently one year of foil and three years of sabre at the American Theatre Wing. There was a local fencing club in Detroit and I was invited to visit their sal-d'arms. I did go and I was invited onto the "strip" (the rubber runner on which one fenced). I had no trouble defeating all comers. Four years schooling in New York with Costello made one an excellent fencer. They asked if I'd come back because their best fencer was out of town for a few days, but he'd be back and they wanted to regain some honor as a fencing academy. I agreed and a few days later, I beat their "expert" fencer handily. When I left, they must have been shaking their heads in utter frustration. That is my only recollection of Detroit, and I've never considered returning.

As usual, the reviews were excellent in Detroit. In fact, in every city, they were good, but none as good as the ones coming up in Chicago, our next stop.

A later *Modern Screen* interview with Peggy Ann said, "Since he [Albert] was over six feet tall, he towered over her. But since when has height got anything to do with love? She slowly fell in love with this tall blond man, who represented the normality she wanted in her life.

"More important to her than movies…more important than the stage or TV…was the dream of holding her first baby in her arms."

Salmi must have sensed that a major life decision was on the horizon, because he telephoned Claire and asked that she meet him at his next stop.

When we got to Chicago, Claire was there. We had a marvelous reunion, spending a great deal of time together.

You wonder about the decisions in life, the personal ones much more than the professional ones. To my mind, personal relationships are the most important things in the world. Professional relationships don't even come a close second.

The opening in Chicago [at the Selwyn theatre] was a personal triumph for me. Claudia Cassidy, the grand dame of reviewers, her reputation known and feared in New York, came, saw, and I conquered. In New York, at that time, a theatre was being renamed the Hayes in honor of Helen Hayes. Claudia Cassidy's review mentioned the renaming of a theatre in New York to the Hayes and suggested in her review that the theatre we were playing be renamed the "Salmi."

She wasn't kidding. I found out later that she had lost a son in the war and my resemblance to him was uncanny. I think maybe she was kind because of that resemblance; nevertheless, the review stood. It was news on both the East and West Coast. [There is now a Claudia Cassidy Theater. It is part of the grand Chicago Cultural Center.]

Late one night, Albert phoned Claire. He wanted to know whether or not they still had a relationship. At that point he was not sure. He asked if she was still his girl. She said no. Years later, he would think back on their times together, feeling a bit sad that he had lost Claire. At the time, though, he realized that he wasn't ready to marry anyone.

While playing in Chicago, I received a telephone call from Josh Logan. He said Twentieth Century-Fox was interested in having me play Bo in their film. The call wasn't a surprise because, before I had left New York on the tour, that talk was already circulating. Paula Strasberg, Lee's wife, had gone so far as to say in print that I was the only one who could play the role. Paula was Marilyn Monroe's mentor, teacher and confidante. This led me to having lunch twice with Marilyn on a one-to-one basis. We spoke of everything but the play and forthcoming movie. Marilyn, at that time, had been made a member of the Actor's Studio. We basically spoke of class work and discussed the scenes we saw at the Studio. She was a delightful girl. I was quite taken by her manner. I had very little interest in doing a "Hollywood film," though. So here was the call from Josh, who was contracted to direct the film Bus Stop, with Monroe starring.

He said Twentieth was definitely interested, and they were offering a seven-year contract to sweeten the deal. I told Josh that 1) I wasn't interested in Hollywood, and 2) I wasn't sure that I even wanted to be an actor for seven more years. What crazy person would turn down a seven-year contract? We talked a little more and he hung up. A few days later, he called again. He said Twentieth would waive the seven-year contract if I agreed to come into New York to screen test. They would pay my fare. Sounded like a good deal to me, so I agreed and, on our first dark night (meaning this day we had off from work; therefore, the theatre was dark), I flew to New York and went to the studio where the screen test was to be filmed, with Josh Logan directing the test. When I got to the studio, I was handed a scene that was written for the film. I got hold of Josh and

asked him if it would be all right if I did the scene from the play in production, rather than the scene from the screenplay. He said it was okay. It put an added pressure on the girl testing with me, for she had learned one script and now quickly had to learn this other one. She did it, we did the test, and I got the first flight back to Chicago. I honestly thought no more of the test and the movie. I had a job, I was content to work in the theatre, and Hollywood could wait forever as far as I was concerned. Footloose and fancy free, that was me.

A few days later, Josh called again. He said that Twentieth looked at the test and their feeling was that I was not right for the role! I had a suitcase full of good reviews and I was not right for the role?

This might be the whole story as far as Albert knew, but there was a lot more to it than that. Jack Garfein, like many others in the business, is sure that it was *Salmi* who did the rejecting. His feeling that "Hollywood could wait forever as far as I was concerned" was apparently communicated to them during the screen test.

Jack Garfein says, "Josh Logan called me one day and he said to me, 'Listen, Jack, I know that you know Albert, and he refuses to do *Bus Stop*. He doesn't want to do *Bus Stop* because 'movies are not art.' I got furious and I called Strasberg, and I knew Strasberg had this relationship with Monroe. 'Listen, this is dangerous what this boy's doing to himself. I mean, what's going on? What is this? He thinks you believe that.' I said, 'Please, Lee, *do* something about it. Call and talk to him.' Lee refused." Strasberg had been quite rough on Salmi and showed no sign of easing up, but Albert continued hold him in high esteem and maintain the lofty philosophy that he espoused. If he had told Salmi to do that movie, he would have done it. Strasberg never called. "I'm furious about this. It was outrageous."

Anyway, our schedule called for us to leave Chicago [after a five-week run] **and from there on in, we had three-night stands until Boston. I left the show before Boston. My contract ran out, and I was tired of three-night stands. I went back to New York.**

While Dick York took over the role of Bo Decker on the road, Salmi moved back into his mother's small apartment at 705 41st Street in Brooklyn and resumed his earlier routine of classes in the daytime and ushering in the evenings.

Back at school, Garfein recalls, "What happened was then he came to the Actors Studio like he used to come, like the young actor who hadn't done anything. He had to start all over. At one point, he criticized a scene in the Studio—I happened to be there—and Lee Strasberg turned on him and said, 'What're you saying? What're you talking about? Well, that's your attitude, and that's why your career is where it is! That's why your career is not moving ahead!' I saw Albert petrified. I mean, he absolutely *believed* in this man, and now that he was 'not a success,' Strasberg turned on him. Since I knew Albert from the very beginning, it was for me kind of a devastating experience. I never got over it."

It appears to have been devastating for Albert, too. His friend Robert Sugarman says, "He came to classes but wouldn't perform. He had developed some sort of grudge against Lee Strasberg as I remember it."

Feeling betrayed by the man he admired was bad enough, but soon another bomb was dropped into Albert's life:

Peggy Ann called me from Boston and told me she was pregnant, and guess who the father was.

I rejoined the Broadway company. [The production had moved now from the Music Box theatre to the Winter Garden.] **Kim Stanley had left the cast, and it seemed every couple weeks I had a new leading lady. Kim was hard to top. We never found one that even came close. On the eighteenth month of the run, a large party was given the cast at the Twenty-One Club, Cillingsly's Place, another theatrical saloon/restaurant. The party was hosted by the producer and Bill Inge; and, for the first time in about eighteen months, Bill spoke to me and we made up. On tour, I discovered that people really loved the play and were deeply touched by it. It was better than a "piece of fluff." I told Bill so. I told him that I had changed my mind about the play, and I apologized for my earlier stupidity. I was truthful, and he accepted my apology.**

That night, we all were the last people to leave the Twenty-One Club, and the next day the management asked that the antlered deer head that was on the wall be returned. I think I know who took it. It was the fellow who played the sheriff. I noticed when he left the club that he had something wrapped in his overcoat, and he owned a rustic cabin in upstate New York. This is the first time I've ever mentioned this incident.

On Albert and Peggy Ann's wedding day – May 18, 1956. *(AP/World Wide Photos)*

Well, the touring company closed in Boston, Peggy Ann came to New York, and I did the right thing. I married her.

Even though they were both in a profession in which multiple marriages were the norm, Salmi saw marriage as a lifetime commitment. R. G. Armstrong was one of the forty guests who attended the wedding, and he felt that Peggy Ann would be good for Albert. "She was solid," he said. They were married on Friday, May 18, 1956, in the First Presbyterian Church by Reverend John B. Macnab, choosing Ina Bernstein and Peter Larkin, their friends from the theatre, to be their attendants.

After a honeymoon in Jamaica, they set up housekeeping. Pat Hingle recalls, "Albert invited Bob Armstrong and me to their place to see what kind of a cook Peggy was. He was acting like a sultan with a slave girl. After a while, she turned on him." Peggy Ann might have gone along with the master-slave act for a little while, but enough was enough. She said, "Get you? Get it yourself!" What had worked for Albert's father was, apparently, not going to cut it for him. This union would be of a more balanced nature than his parents' had been. It was then that Albert's two friends realized "Yeah! Peggy's *all right!*" She could handle Albert just fine.

The couple was also visited by Peggy's aunt and uncle, Jeanne and Vince DeVito, Sr. Their apartment, Vince says, was "quite drab. I kept thinking that they could have afforded something better. If my memory serves me, the apartment was a very large open room for living and sleeping quarters and an enclosed alcove for the kitchen."

Catherine Ann Salmi was born on March 30, 1957—ten months after her parents' wedding. Had Garner been mistaken about having been pregnant when she called from Boston? Had she tried to deceive Salmi? We can only speculate.

Nevertheless, Albert and Peggy Ann were now the parents of a golden-haired baby daughter, who brought more responsibility to their lives. To family members, little Catherine's initials became her nickname, and they called her "Cas" or "Cassie." Her more affectionate name, however, was "Kitten."

Motherhood seemed to agree with Peggy Ann, and she sent an excited letter about it to Virginia: "You have a lovely granddaughter—3 weeks old this morn. Her name is Catherine Ann Salmi, and she has blond hair and blue eyes (which I hope don't change) She weighed 5 lbs., 15 oz. and came 3 weeks early—on March 30th, at 10:25 a.m. She was due around April 22nd, but she's here all safe and sound, and we're delighted! The day she was born, I woke about 6:30 in the morn and thought I had a terrible gas pain and tried to get back to sleep, but couldn't. Albert woke and made me call the doctor, who in turn said 'Go to the hospital.' At 10:25 a.m. we had a baby girl! I was a bit worried about her being early, but thank God, she's healthy and beautiful as can be."

Neither had had experience with babies, each of them having been an only child. He was willing to learn, though. In an interview with *Modern Screen*, Peggy Ann recalled, "When we brought Cas home, she was so tiny I was afraid to give her a bath. Albert gave Cas her first bath."

Pat Hingle, who was also a father now, had been able to help his friend here. "I was the one who taught Albert how to diaper his baby. At first, he was afraid she would break."

Peggy's letter to her mother continues, "We had a nurse who stayed for two weeks. She left yesterday, thank God—as she was really becoming a menace. Yesterday, last night, today, and now tonight we finally have the baby to ourselves—and boy, I'm exhausted! She's on a three-hour schedule, which makes it kinda rough. Albert is sleeping now, and he takes over in a couple of hours. Then I sleep for awhile, and vice-versa.

"Guess I'm prejudiced, but she was the prettiest baby in the hospital nursery—even the nurses agreed!"

Their friend Mark Richman recalls, "She was a pale little blonde, lovely girl, very well dressed out."

We lived on 28th, off Lexington, in the Murryhill district, a Sanford White built building. Next door to our apartment house was a little theatre, gone now, torn down, named The Davenport theatre, owned and operated by Mr. Davenport, who directed and starred in all the productions. He was about seventy or eighty years old and played everything. His memory was failing, so he would have the lines hidden all over the stage. He referred to them in such an obvious manner that he was considered a cute oddity.

Soon, Albert had another stage job - the play entitled *The Good Woman of Setzuan*. From this play came a new friendship with actor Zero Mostel. Says Robert Sugarman, "He became friendly with Zero who, at that point, was blacklisted and had lost all his movie, TV, and nightclub work. Zero was also a painter and I remember that once a week Al would go to Zero's studio in New York's flower district to play cards with him, which was a terrific thing to do as Zero was so isolated."

The Salmis had an active social life with friends dropping by frequently. One couple they both enjoyed was Mark Richman and his wife, Helen. "They would come to our place for dinner," Richman recalls. "We had an apartment in New York on West 20th Street." The men would see each other frequently at the Actors Studio and elsewhere. Paul Newman and his wife Joanne Woodward would also have the Salmis over for dinner occasionally.

Live TV was healthy in New York during this period, and I had a show practically every week.

With a family now to support, Salmi continued to supplement his income by doing live TV broadcasts regularly. Most well-known of all these roles was one that he had done six months before his daughter's birth when he played Bruce Pearson in *The United States Steel Hour's* "Bang

Paul Newman, George Peppard and Salmi in the 1956 live TV broadcast of
Bang the Drum Slowly. (Photofest)

the Drum Slowly," televised on September 26, 1956. Paul Newman and
Salmi played the main characters in what was to become a classic that
defined "the Golden Age of Television."

The following year, the Harcourt Brace Awards honored the seven
best television plays of 1957. Included in the top seven was the *U.S. Steel
Hour*'s "Survival," starring Albert Salmi.

Chapter Three

"Maybe once I've made my pile, I'll just write for you to come and help me spend it."

– Albert Salmi as Chuck Mathers
The Fugitive, "Angels Travel on Lonely Roads"

Salmi loved working on Broadway, but it was not enough to keep him busy full time. After years in which he resisted the big screen, he finally accepted an important role.

My agent got a call from MGM, asking if I was available to do a film entitled *The Brothers Karamazov*. I had been working at the Studio on the Brothers with an actor named Stefan Gierasch. We were doing a scene from that piece of classic literature. Stefan was working on the character I eventually did in the film, while I was working on the character that Bill Shatner did in the film. I accepted right away. I mean this was not some hackneyed script—we were going to do a classic. A dream come true! I was excited by the prospect of the coming work.

I was flown out to L.A. by MGM and was given a little studio apartment near MGM, walking distance away. I went to the studio to meet the director, Richard Brooks. The first person I saw was the receptionist, who had difficulty believing I was who I said I was. She ushered me in to see Brooks' personal secretary and, again, I was questioned. The secretary said that they had all thought that I was a short, dark Italian. Here standing before her was a tall, blond Finn. She kind of shrugged her shoulders and told me to go through a door to Mr. Brooks' office. Same thing from Mr. Brooks. He said that I had been represented as a short, dark Italian. I told him I made no such representation, my agent certainly didn't, and wherever did he get such an idea? He explained that they originally had wanted the English actor Herbert Lom, a short, dark Italian; but, because of political reasons, he could not get into the United States. Brooks had mentioned this to another director, Marty Ritt. Coincidentally, Marty and I were old coffee-drinking pals in New York. Well, Marty said, "Get Albert Salmi. He'd be perfect for it." Brooks took his advice, but he assumed that, since Marty knew Lom was unavailable, Marty would suggest someone about the same size and coloring. There I was in his office and, to his credit, he said, "Okay. We'll go with you." I signed the contract, got the script, went to costume fittings and did everything necessary to begin work. I was set in the part, but the Lom ghost was still to haunt me.

The first day on the set, the producer, Pandro Berman, came up to me, introduced himself and asked me if I was aware that this script was taken from classic literature. I assured him that I was well acquainted with the work. He then told me he didn't want a western accent from the character. He obviously knew about *The Rainmaker* and *Bus Stop*. I told him that I had been born and bred in New York and had spent very little time in the west. He started to leave, changed his mind, looked at me again and said, "We don't want a New York accent either!"

In his first scene to be filmed, Salmi was experimenting with a particular accent to see how it would work. It seemed more Mexican than Russian, though. Maybe he'd better try it a different way. Too late! The director liked the scene and that's the one he would use in the finished picture, so Salmi had to continue using that accent for the rest of the filming. He learned then that a film actor isn't able to experiment the way a stage actor is.

The first really kind words came from Yul Brynner. He came up to me, called me by name, and said that he was not an actor but more of a personality, and he was relying on me and the other cast members to carry him. Whether he meant it or not, he certainly made me feel accepted.

The Brothers Karamazov, MGM.

I knew other members of the cast, having worked with them. Among them was Lee J. Cobb, whom I liked very much and had worked with before. We worked together later on *The Virginian*, a western TV series. He was a regular on that series. From TV to a classical piece of writing. One just never knew what was around the corner.

He was also working with his Dramatic Worship friend Gloria Pall, who appeared early in the film as the bound woman being tickled with a feather in the orgy scene, while Albert's character, Smerdjakov, looked on disapprovingly. Gloria had made the move to Hollywood in 1951.

The Brothers Karamazov was the first of several films that he would do with William Shatner (his film debut), whose first impression of Albert had been that of a warm and loving person. "The longer I knew him, the more charming he was," he said. "He was a good fellow and a superb actor."

Among many humorous anecdotes of their working relationship, Shatner recalls, "I remember vaguely a tame bear that went wild because the trainer didn't have his bottle of Coke and Albert did, so the bear went after Albert, the trainer went after the bear, and I went after the trainer because she was beautiful. The whole thing was quite a mess." He says that in all the times they worked together, he saw evidence of Albert's temper only that one time. "When the bear got a hold of him, he got very upset.

"I noticed one particular habit that made me very watchful of him. He kept knocking over bottles of soda, wine, water. Whenever there was a bottle near him, he'd knock it over."

The work that Stefan had done on the character was of great help to me. We worked long hours and hard, and soon the picture was finished.

Richard Brooks became a friend, I think, because of the work I did in the picture. Perhaps he was relieved that I had worked out so well. Before I flew back to New York, he had me over for dinner at his house. As the evening wore on, he told me MGM was going to put me up for an Oscar in the supporting role category. He said vehemently for me to not accept, as this would be the kiss of death professionally. I listened to what he said. I didn't believe what he was saying, but, if it should come to pass, I certainly would consider his advice. After all, he had much more experience about Hollywood than I did.

Jack Garfein feels Albert's Smerdjakov, was very much like Albert himself. Smerdjakov idolized his brother and would do anything to please him, even if doing so would jeopardize his own future—and that was how Salmi felt about Lee Strasberg. "Idealizing him and carrying out his wishes," Garfein said. "To me, that's what happened with Albert, the tragedy."

Back to New York to resume Studio classes and be with the family. The picture came out and was well received, and MGM did call to ask if I would accept an Oscar nomination for best supporting actor. I was still very much New York and theatre oriented, so I told the caller that I didn't think it fair for me to be nominated for one picture. I said that I felt Oscars should be presented to actors who have

shown a large body of work of a high quality, and that one picture does not an Oscar winner make. He thanked me for my time and hung up. I heard no more about the Oscar. I was stupid, again. How many times can an actor self-destruct?

Live television ceased and the TV work shifted to the west coast. Peggy was homesick for California. We had the money and, through her persuasion, we moved to California. I would have preferred to live in New York, but I didn't really drag my feet. So California, here we came.

In a Twentieth Century-Fox pressbook interview Salmi said, "The dough is here—on the movie sound stages. Any actor who claims the high salaries didn't intrigue or lure him out here is uttering falsehoods through his pearly dentures. Nothing can ever change my feeling and devotion for the stage. Working in front of a camera can't compare to the thrill you get performing before a live audience."

We rented houses in the Brentwood section of Los Angeles for a few years…

Perhaps Albert was renting houses, rather than buying one, with the thought that this move would not be permanent. To put down roots might have felt to him like he was giving up on New York. After living in California a while, he realized he just did not like Hollywood. It seemed so phony to him.

In New York, public transportation was everywhere, but they were in California now, where such services were not as convenient. Until he had time to get his driver's license, Peggy Ann was his chauffeur, rising at 6 a.m. to take him to the studio, and picking him up at the end of the workday.

In a letter, Peggy Ann told her mother, "We have a lovely house, with a wonderful backyard, which will be great for the baby in the summertime. We have flowers and a few fruit trees, which Albert loves. I looked at about thirty houses before finding this one, but it was worth waiting for.

"Last Monday, Albert finished the last shot of the film [*The Bravados*] and was running to the car and tripped and fell, and broke his arm in two places. He is in a cast and in terrible pain. The cast will remain on for several weeks and, of course, it's the left arm, and he is left-handed. He was supposed to have started rehearsal for *Climax* last Tuesday, but, needless to say, was unable to."

Peggy Ann and Salmi's new home on Burlingame in Los Angeles.

"I'd heard about actors getting a break in Hollywood," Salmi joked in the *Bravados* pressbook. "Man, I got mine after my second picture."

We finally bought a house on Bundy Drive, just up from Joe E. Brown's home.

Once his arm healed, Salmi was able to do a 1958 *Climax!* episode entitled "The Volcano Seat," in which he co-starred with Michael Rennie. This seems to be the show he's describing in his memoir:

I'd like to relate a tale of live TV in which I starred with a man who was also highly regarded as an actor. Basically, the plot was of the in-flight fueling of other aircraft. We were the fuel plane and, during one fueling, the fuel bulkhead was punctured and we had to bring the plane in very slowly and totally level. If the plane wasn't level, if the nose was up, the liquid fuel would run to the tail and we would stall and go down tail first. If the nose of the plane was down, the fuel would slosh forward and we would dive to our deaths. It was a simple story, and, coupled with stock shots of the plane in flight, we could carry out the story believably.

We rehearsed three weeks first the fueling of fighter planes. They got into a row and one by one came in, hooked up, got the fuel un-

hooked, and the next plane took its place. Then the accident! Then the tense, careful flying to land, staying level all the way. Finally, braking very slowly on landing to prevent the gasoline from slamming forward. We would have little scenes and then go to the stock shot showing the plane in flight, then in the studio another scene, gingerly leveling the plane, watching the speed, then the stock shot of the plane, then the scene in the studio of turning slowly and level to return to the field, then the stock shot of the plane turning, then back to the studio explaining to the control tower our problem, back to stock shot, then in the cockpit where the two men speak of their lives and their dreams, then the stock shot of the plane. This goes on and on for an hour, and we finally land safely and the tower says, "Well done."

The technical rehearsal went very well. It was stop-and-go to make sure all the ducks were in a row, lighting good, shadows good, projection of sky and clouds good, handling of instruments good, everything fine. We broke for dinner, then back to the studio and into the realistic mock-up of the plane's cockpit for the dress rehearsal. This began with the normal "ten seconds, nine, eight, seven, six, five, four, three, two," and then the floor manager points and we begin the play. This we did. We played the first little scene, then we knew they went to the stock shot of the plane, then the signal from the floor manager, we played the next scene, and so on.

About five minutes into the play, I saw the director come rushing from the control room in a highly agitated way, waving his arms like a demented dervish. My fellow actor and I were astounded and we slid back the cockpit window. We, at first, could not hear what he was saying because of the engine noise, which, of course, was recorded and had not been cut off. Finally, someone cut the engine recording and there stood the director looking up at this mock-up of the plane's cockpit with tears in his eyes, and the words we finally heard were, "Aren't you going to act for me?" The other actor and I exchanged incredulous stares. We were convinced that the director had lost his mind.

We finally got the story from him. When they cut to us in the cockpit, we were just sitting there, doing nothing. Then went to stock, they came back to us and there we were, sitting there doing and saying nothing. What had happened was in the initial opening of the dress rehearsal, we misunderstood the floor manager's finger pointing. As it happens, we were playing the scene when they were showing the stock

Playing the lead in *Peter Hurkos*.

shots and sitting quietly when they were on us. In live TV, the camera that was operating exhibited a red light so the actor knew which camera was live. However, because of the large amount of glass in the plane's windshields, the red lights were disconnected, so we were relying totally on the floor manager. We really could not look at him directly, so we got our cue from large, sweeping arm movements and these we read incorrectly. There was very little time left before the show was to air, so all we did was talk to the floor manager to make sure that we were perfectly clear as to his cues. We assured the director that there would be no more

problems. We did the show, everything went swimmingly, scenes played, stock shots, we came to the end, breathed a sigh of relief, got out of our costumes, and went home. Such was the life of a live TV actor.

Because of the time differences throughout the country, the show was broadcast live on one coast, then the live tape was shown a few hours later on the west coast.

We did the show and three hours later, we watched ourselves. It was always a great way to get a girl into your apartment. "Come on up and see my etchings." It never failed.

In July, 1958, Salmi and his wife found themselves working together again, this time in the *Westinghouse Studio One* production "Man Under Glass." Unfortunately for Peggy Ann, her husband was soon off to the east coast, again, cast in another play, *Howie*. He played the title character, who had just been discharged from the Navy and was in search of a career. Mounted at the 46th Street Theatre on Broadway, it co-starred Leon Ames, Peggy Conklin, Patricia Smith, Patricia Bosworth, Nicholas Pryor and Gene Saks. The November, 1958, *Theatre Arts* magazine reported, "None of the seven newspaper judges had praise for the play, though the performers, especially Mr. Salmi, were well received."

Howie was also presented at the Wilbur Theatre in Boston, across the street from where his friend William Shatner was performing at that time. In *Howie*'s audience one night was Irja Helen's daughter Nancy. A teenager now, Nancy was invited backstage and would finally get to know this man of whom her mother was so fond. "He was very handsome and imposing. Very tall, very blond, and very Finnish looking." She found him to be "humble and sincere, which I attribute to the nature of a Finn, the characteristic that struck me on my trips to Finland as well as with my associations with Finns in this country. I remember too when I complimented him on his acting talents that he commented that Peggy was the real talent, having been in the business much longer than he. He felt that a marriage relationship was so important, and he was so hopeful that this marriage would be lifelong," she says.

At the 29th National Board of Review Awards presentation in 1958, both *The Brothers Karamazov* and Salmi had been nominated. The film lost to *The Old Man and the Sea*, but Salmi won for Best Supporting Actor for his work in *The Brothers Karamazov* and *The Bravados*. Also sharing the stage to receive their awards were Spencer Tracy as Best Actor, Ingrid Bergman as Best Actress, and Kay Walsh as Best Supporting Actress.

I was hired to co-star with Gable and Lancaster in the film *Run Silent, Run Deep*. Seek not for me in that film. The producers were [Harold] **Hecht**, [James] **Hill** and Lancaster. I saw Heckt. He handed me the script and said, "Welcome aboard." In those days, it was so, so simple. I had just had a successful picture that I was very good in. This can be disastrous for an actor in Tinseltown. Your head has a tendency to grow a bit and logic flies out the window. The first day, I had an eight- or ten-page scene with Clark Gable. Just Clark and me. All day.

Early in the morning, I was sitting in the make-up chair and the director, Bob Wise, came in. Without saying hello or anything nice, he said, "Albert, Gable isn't feeling good today, so don't make any waves." A warning, if I ever heard one. I thought, "to hell with him and Gable." I had a job to do and I was going to do it. That's what I thought. Then I got on the set. The scene took place in an office with Gable, as the officer, sitting behind a desk and me in front of the desk, filling him in on how dangerous this submarine mission we were going on was—an enlisted man telling an officer. The information had to be put on the table so the audience could understand what we were about to do. It was all expositional with strange, hard-to-pronounce names and a lot of technical stuff. I can understand why I got the lines. The "King" didn't want them.

Before we started, Wise pointed out marks on the floor for me to stand on, and to move to, and to move again to another, and on and on. The marks looked like a wild checkerboard. I told Wise that he ought to have the stand-in who formed this crazy quilt of marks to play the scene since he had already orchestrated it. This did not endear me to anyone on the set. It took us all morning to get the master shot. I felt like a jumping jack, going from one mark to another. The marks are necessary in film work, for the camera has to know where the actor is going, the lighting has to be level at all the stopping marks, and the marks help in focusing the lens because the distance from the lens to the mark is pre-measured so the image will always be sharp. The actor playing the part, in conjunction with the director, moves with his instincts to form the marks that are used. Wise opted to do it ass-backwards, because Gable wasn't feeling well.

Gable didn't look well, either. He was not the perfect picture of a blood-and-guts submarine commander. His shaking head put me off dreadfully. The man sitting in front of me was a sham. I gave no indication of my anger at the marks and at my discomfort acting with an ailing actor. I couldn't understand how they could use the master. I felt I was spinning my wheels. The only part of the master they could use was my making an entrance into the office and my exit from the office. The scene would have to be close-ups. We broke for lunch and I was very unhappy. When we returned from lunch, they were lighting for the close-up; Gable's close-up. I was sitting about three feet from Gable and we were making small talk. Then Wise came over to me and said that Gable's contract limits his time at work and that's why his close-up was being done first. After his close-up, he was going to leave, and Wise asked if it were all right if the script girl read his part to me for my close-up. I said in a voice too loud, "Sure, fine, but, for crying out loud, get an actor." They did get an actor to read Gable's lines, but the damage had been done. We finished Gable's and my close-ups, and I went home for the day.

The next day, I went to work. I entered my dressing room and all my costumes had been removed. Now I knew they weren't removed for cleaning, but it really didn't hit me yet. Nothing was going on. On the stage, it was strangely quiet. In one corner of the stage, there seemed to be a rehearsal going on. The actors were new. One new actor was reading the part of my friend in the picture. I went to find my friend and tell him of my discovery. I found him eating breakfast on the lot, and I told him he'd better get back to the stage because someone was rehiring his part. He said he would go to the stage when he finished breakfast. I said I'd have a cup of coffee and go back with him. Eventually, he finished his breakfast and we started for the stage. He said he had to make a pit stop and went into the men's room. I told him I'd wait for him. He never came out, or I missed him, but a half-hour was a long time to wait; so I went back to the stage and went into my dressing room. The dressing room was a portable one and was located against the stage wall. I left the door open so I could see when things got into gear. After a while, I saw my agent, Heckt and Hill come walking toward my dressing room. They all entered my dressing room, and my agent said, "It doesn't work, Albert."

I still didn't get it. "What doesn't work?"

"You, in the role. You're being replaced."

Heckt and Hill left after the "we're sorrys" were exchanged. When they were gone, I turned to my agent and said, "Am I paid?" meaning my salary. He assured me I was. Then he suggested I say goodbye to Burt Lancaster and to Clark Gable. I had no intention of saying goodbye to Gable, but I did say goodbye to Burt. As I was leaving the stage, I glanced over to my dressing room and there was the actor I had warned going over his new role. I went up to the door of the dressing room and asked him if he would like me to "cue" him, as I was up on the part. He didn't know what to say. He said he was told not to say anything about what was going on, so that's why he ducked me. That's how Jack Warden played the role I was originally cast in. Win some, lose some.

Years later, Salmi told a reporter that things had turned out for the best. He felt that he wasn't equipped to handle a career as demanding as those that the stars have. He had seen what complicated and difficult lives they had, and he did not want to live that way. Soon he had established himself as a character actor and was being seen in films and on television regularly.

Salmi returned to New York to star in a Broadway revival of the H. R. Lenormand play, *The Failures*. He and Peggy McCay played the leads. In his review, Brooks Atkinson wrote, "It is also likely that Albert Salmi is not happily cast as the husband and playwright. Mr. Salmi is an uncommonly interesting actor who has force and color—almost local color. But there is a naivete about his style that goes badly with the tensions of the part he is playing now." The show lived up to its name and did not enjoy a long or successful run.

Albert was more in his element when, in 1960, he guest starred for the first of four times on the highly popular *Bonanza*. No longer plagued by an overly boyish appearance, he was now often cast as the sinister tough guy. Also that year, he made the first of three guest appearances on *The Twilight Zone*, cast as a man about to be hanged who is instantly transported to the present-day. Marc Scott Zicree writes in his book *The Twilight Zone Companion*, "Playing nineteenth-century killer Joe Caswell was Albert Salmi, a fine character actor who deserves better roles than he usually gets. Here, he gives Caswell an air of authenticity, speaking with an archaic accent and moving with the menacing body language of a man long used to violence. His is a faultless performance, but it is not enough to overcome a poorly adapted script."

As Charlie Rawlins in *The Unforgiven*, with a young Audrey Hepburn.
(Salmi family collection)

Salmi did most of his own stunts in that episode. In one scene, he escaped a modern-day telephone booth by falling backwards through the glass and landing on the ground. This was all done in one continuous take, so it was obvious that the actor had done it himself when he then turned over and stood up. He had probably broken the glass with his back so that any bruises

The Unforgiven, with John Saxon.

that might result wouldn't be visible in other scenes. Co-star Russell Johnson says that he and Albert did the fight scene themselves, as well.

Albert and Peggy Ann were now expecting another child, but while they were in Mexico for his work on the film *The Unforgiven*, she became quite ill with dysentery and suffered a miscarriage.

The couple was able to work together again the following year in the 1961 *Naked City* episode, "Button in the Haystack." Salmi played an innocent man wrongfully accused of murder, and Garner played his loving and supportive wife.

Their characters' relationship on this show was unshakable. In real life, however, it was otherwise. She yearned for the professional respect and the quality roles that had been so accessible to her earlier, but it just wasn't happening. An example of this is in the annual magazine called *Who's Who in Hollywood*. In the 1960s, it listed Salmi, but not his wife. Conflict and resentment was inevitable. Salmi told a friend that his being away from home so much, working on location, was probably the reason for Peggy Ann's unhappiness. She had given up roles that would have kept them apart, but he had accepted work regardless of location. It's true that, when they were apart, they had written loving letters to each other; but that just wasn't enough.

With Lee Remick, in *Wild River*.

They separated on February 16, 1961.

He then returned to New York and was cast in *Once There Was a Russian* on Broadway, at the Music Box Theatre—the same stage on which he had made his first mark in *Bus Stop*. The down side was being so far away from his little daughter.

Unfortunately, *Once There Was a Russian* closed after only one performance. The ensemble then presented the play elsewhere, including the National Theatre in Washington, DC, and the Playhouse Theatre in Wilmington, Delaware. Starring with Salmi in this comedy were Walter Matthau, Francoise Rosay, and Julie Newmar.

Garner filed for divorce in August, charging Albert with cruelty that had caused her "mental suffering, anguish and distress." She explained that she had neck pain and thyroid problems because their arguments would cause her to become tense. What arguments? Albert thoroughly disliked Hollywood and wanted to move back to New York, where stage opportunities were best, and where his widowed mother lived. Peggy Ann wanted to stay in California, where their film opportunities were better. While she was telling reporters that she believed the husband should be the undisputed head of the household, that wasn't the philosophy by which she was living.

Their divorce was dated March 13, 1963. They both agreed that Peggy Ann would have custody of five-year-old Cas. It would have been difficult for him to care for a child while travelling so much, anyway. They also agreed on the settlement—Albert would pay Peggy Ann $200/month child support until Cas was twenty-one, $100/month alimony for three years, and $250 attorney's fees. Garner told interviewers that she and Salmi had parted with no animosity.

A month later, television viewers saw for the first time a classic *Twilight Zone* episode entitled "Of Late, I Think of Cliffordville." Salmi's was the main character, William J. Feathersmith, a ruthless tycoon who, after staying late at his office and encountering custodian Hecate (played by Wright King), yearns for the days when he was building his empire. It's the *getting* of it that was "the kick", not the *having* of it. Feathersmith makes a deal with the devil (played by Julie Newmar) to go back in time to his youth and relive his exciting rise to the top. Things go awry, however, and when he returns to the present day, he discovers that *he's* now the humble custodian while Hecate is the tycoon.

What was it like on the set of that production? Wright King tells us that Salmi joyously confided in him that he would be marrying a nurse soon.

What a fine union that would be! Like Peggy Ann, most nurses are very caring, loving people.

Albert Salmi and Wright King in *The Twilight Zone*

Chapter Four

"I've been traveling for over a week. A man likes a woman
to be waiting when he gets back."
— Albert Salmi as Albie
Bonanza, "Silent Thunder"

In 1962, Salmi had been invited to a dinner party by the wife of his
friend Darren McGavin, with whom he had co-starred on Broadway in
The Rainmaker. At that party, a beautiful and animated woman named
Roberta Taper caught his eye. She resembled Claire, and he learned that
Roberta was the niece of Darren's wife.

Albert was a towering 6'2", Roberta was a petite 5'2". They were
opposites in many other ways, as well. He was Christian, she was Jewish.
He was as reserved as she was outgoing, but she had a little-girl quality
that he found endearing, and a spunkiness that he admired. She also had
a mischievous streak that amused him.

They had some things in common, though—a love for tennis, a
delicious sense of humor, and a variety of interests. Bright and articulate,
Roberta was to be the love of Albert's life. At that time, however, she had
recently married financier and philanthropist S. Mark Taper, who was
thirty-four years her senior; and Albert's divorce was not yet final.

Taper was quite an accomplished man, and being his wife was very
prestigious. His long and productive marriage to his first wife, Amelia,
ended when she died in 1958. Four years later, he had taken a new bride,
Roberta Gail Pollock Morris. This marriage, however, was not a happy
one.

Salmi as the title character in the "Brother Thaddeus" episode of *The Virginian.*

Salmi was now living on Pacific View Drive in Hollywood and his agent, MCA, was approached by award-winning producer Norman Felton about a pilot for a television series called *Grand Slam.* He would guest star as a baseball catcher who tried for the major leagues, failed, then returned to the minors. The show would focus on the adjustment that he and his young son faced. Felton wanted it done right so it would sell for the 1963-64 season. Director Buzz Kulik and Albert as the guest star were his first choices.

For the six days of work, Albert was paid $2,500.00. When it was finished, producer Felton wrote in a memo to Kulik, "Buzz, one never knows whether a project will 'go' in our business, but each time I view *Grand Slam* I feel very, very proud of it." Still, it failed to sell.

As time went on, Roberta's and Albert's marital circumstances changed. She now stated that her marriage to Mark Taper had been annulled. The Taper family seems to have a different understanding of what took place, however. According to his December 16, 1994, *Los Angeles Times* obituary, Taper had sued her for divorce only eight months after their marriage had begun, claiming that Roberta had married him "for the sole and exclusive purpose of obtaining monetary gain." The termination of their marriage is dated February 27, 1963.

Salmi and second wife Roberta Taper.
(Salmi family collection)

Seven months later, Roberta gave birth to a daughter, Elizabeth Anne. Perhaps it was because of this that the press seems to have thought Albert and Roberta were married. Larry Quirk's Hollywood-New York column in the March, 1964, issue of *Movies Magazine* states, "Albert Salmi has a naughty face, but that is mighty deceptive. He's a solid family man; only woman in his life is wife Roberta." His faithfulness to

Albert and Roberta's first child, Lizanne.
(Salmi family collection)

With Fess Parker and Ed Ames on *Daniel Boone*. *(Photofest)*

Roberta was apparently common knowledge, but the report of marriage was a bit premature. In fact, according to Peggy's mother, Albert was having "woman problems" now and had had a paternity suit filed against him.

The Report of Final Decree of Divorce for Albert and Peggy Ann was issued on April 3, 1964. Peggy Ann would marry Kenyon Foster Brown that August. Salmi bought a lovely house at 243 Oceano Drive in the Brentwood section of Los Angeles. The next day, Saturday, April 25th, he and Roberta were wed. Performing the ceremony in Los Angeles was Rabbi William M. Kramer. Joan and Marvin Birdt were their attendants.

This was to be the last and most enduring of twenty-nine-year-old Roberta's three marriages and thirty-six-year-old Albert's two.

While she had done some acting and modeling under the name Roberta Gayle in the past, and later was an agent for a brief time, she considered herself a housewife and was now content to devote herself to helping Salmi in his career. While he concentrated on his work, books, plays, and art, Roberta took over management of their finances. She would often be seen on the set as he was working, and at home, she helped him find the peace and quiet he needed to study his roles effectively, and she shared and supported his interests.

It turned out, though, that multimillionaire Mark Taper was a hard act to follow. Salmi soon discovered that he and his new wife were opposites in yet another way—he was thrifty, she was a big spender. In his previous marriage, Peggy Ann had been working, too, so there was not as much pressure on him to generate a high income in that marriage as there was in this one. That might be why most of his award-winning work was done early in his career, when he was free to hold out for quality roles. Now, he had to be less discriminating in the parts he accepted.

Fortunately, in 1964, he began work on a brand new television series, *Daniel Boone*, playing the lead character's unsophisticated and sometimes quite humorous buddy, Carolina E. Yadkin. Salmi received billing second to Fess Parker, who played the lead.

The show was quite a hit, and soon related products began showing up on the market. There was a monthly Daniel Boone comic book, a View-Master episode in 3-D, sheet music of the show's theme song and many others. Images of Albert and his Boonesboro cohabitants were showing up everywhere.

Ed Ames, who played scholarly native-American Mingo on the show, recalls, "Albert had long, blond hair at the time. A man drove up behind him and blew his horn and uttered expletives. The man dared Albert to stop and pull over. Albert did and, when he got out of the car—all six feet plus of him—the man gunned his car and fled."

Salmi, according to co-star Dallas McKennon, "always seemed so at ease in his close-ups, so popular with cast and crew alike on the set." Nevertheless, he stayed with *Daniel Boone* for only the 1964-65 season. Why? With Albert's typical honesty, he explains in a letter to a fan: "Dear Mrs. Stutzman, I wish I could go on acting 'Yadkin' for you this year but the sponsors don't want me. Yours, Albert Salmi." Perhaps it was a finan-

The Ambushers, 1967. *(Photofest)*

cial decision. In the first season, the main character had two sidekicks - Yadkin and Mingo. Why pay two when most shows have just one? Ed Ames, as Mingo, had a huge fan base, so that probably had a bearing on which character to keep.

In June, 1965, his youngest daughter Jennifer Lee was born with a serious heart defect. A child with this problem is commonly referred to as a "blue baby". She was placed in an incubator, and the doctors offered very little hope that she would survive. Jenny steadfastly held her own and eventually grew strong enough to come home.

One TV role that year was in *The Virginian* episode, "A Little Learning." His was a very intense, but tender and gentle, character. Series star James Drury recalls it vividly: "He was just the nicest person you'd ever want to be around. He's a very interesting guy. He had a really high, high level of intelligence and he was extremely interested in lots of different things." To offset the rigors of the fourteen-hour days needed to film this ninety-minute show, the set was a very upbeat one. Salmi fit right in. "He was the life of the party," Drury says. "He always had new jokes."

The following year, Salmi made up for lost time with numerous television appearances, some of which were among his most memorable.

With Susan Oliver *The Virginian* episode, "A Little Learning."

The 1966 *Big Valley* episode "Under a Dark Star" is considered by many to be one of his most impressive works ever.

Also that year, he guest starred in the *Lost in Space* episode, "The Sky Pirate" that lingers in many of his fans' memories to this day. This offbeat role must have been like a breath of fresh air. His eyes sparkled as he played Alonzo P. Tucker—a whimsical, likable pirate with a robotic, smart-mouthed parrot on his shoulder. It was a lighthearted epi-

Albert Salmi's portrait of wife Roberta.
(Jennifer LaRue)

sode that showcased Albert's ability to project subtle, gentle humor. This became one of Albert's all-time favorite guest roles. He described Tucker as "very imaginative and a lot of fun to act out. It was a role that seldom came along."

As always, he developed this character himself. Jonathan Harris said that the idea of the lower, more throaty voice was Albert's; and Dan Petrie, Sr. (who directed him in several different projects) agreed that the man would just plow forth, carrying out his ideas about such things without discussing them first. Albert made this lovable character uniquely his own, and the casting could not have been more perfect. He even invited Aune Luttio, the sister of his housekeeper, Viola Lepisto, over to the set to watch the fun.

Later that year, he appeared in the revival of Eugene O'Neill's play *Anna Christie*, directed by his Actors Studio friend, Jack Garfein. The set designer was Peter Larkin, who had served as attendant at Albert's first wedding back in New York. Salmi, Carroll Baker, and James Whitmore performed this play at the Hartford Theatre in Hollywood. At this point in his life, it appears that Albert was making a point to stay close to home.

One of his other creative outlets was painting, including portraits of his wife, Roberta. The same attention to detail that he gave to his work is also evident in his art. "He was an incredible artist," their daughter, Jenny, later told *The Spokesman-Review*, "a technically correct artist." For some reason, though, he gave the hobby up, which was a big disappointment to Jenny in later years. "He was an artist in his heart. That's where I think I got some of my desire to do artwork."[2] Cas, too, inherited this talent.

The next year, 1967, brought Salmi an award that he would cherish more than any other. The National Cowboy Hall of Fame presented him with their Wrangler Award at their seventh annual Western Heritage Awards

[2] *The Spokesman-Review*, "Salmi's space offering a means of expression for artists and children", by Dan Webster (2/16/95)

ceremony on April 14th for his work on the January 8, 1966, *Gunsmoke* episode, "Death Watch." The presentation took place in the Persian Room of the Skirvin Tower Hotel in Oklahoma City. The trophy was an original bronze sculpture of a cowboy on horseback, created by artist John Free. The first of these awards were presented in 1960; and *Gunsmoke*, which had already been running for five years at that point, hadn't received one until this point in its eleventh season. The episode also won awards for the regular cast members, the writer, producers, and director.

Unfortunately, Roberta's hot temper was making life difficult at home. Just in the nick of time once he ducked a large crystal vase hurtling through the air toward his head. He had scars to mark the times his reflexes hadn't been as fast. "I'm scared to death of her," he would say, only half jokingly.

I was hired to do a picture to be shot up in Santa Barbara and in Los Angeles. I knew the director fairly well, and the actors also hired I knew by reputation. There were a few reading rehearsals, and we saw the sets in L.A. We were going up to Santa Barbara around July 7th; but on July 4th, I went to play tennis with the director at the house of another director, whose brother also was a director. The four of us played and were very competitive—so competitive that in my desire to win, no matter what, I didn't clear the court of a tennis ball, which I then stepped on, turning my ankle. I went down in a heap. I asked that we have a time out so I could tape up the ankle and have a drink before continuing. We all had a drink and sat around for a while. My ankle started to swell and was painful to walk on, so I bid my adieus, walked to my car and drove home.

I kidded around a great deal with my wife and, when she saw me come limping into the house, she offered no sympathy and told me to stop clowning around. I went into the den and poured another drink. The ankle was really hurting and really beginning to swell. When my wife came into the den and saw the ankle, she said, "You're going to a doctor." I said it was only sprained, but with the filming beginning soon, I'd better have it attended to. I began sweating at the possibility that the ankle was indeed broken. I told my wife that we couldn't find a doctor on the 4th of July on a bet. Our doctor had left on his phone the number of a substitute doctor, whom we called. He said to meet him at his office and he could have an x-ray taken of the ankle, then he would proceed accordingly. We went to his Beverly

Hills office, he examined the ankle, twisting, turning it, having me move my toes. He said since I was in the office, what would it hurt to have an x-ray. I agreed, and a half-hour later he told me I had broken my ankle! Goodbye, film. Goodbye, good salary. Actually, I didn't like the film. I didn't like my role in the film, so I've always thought that perhaps subconsciously I hurt myself so I wouldn't have to do it. (The film itself, when it finally was released, was a disaster and disappeared quickly.) The doctor put a cast on the ankle, gave me crutches and sent me home.

On arriving back at the house, I knew it was my duty to alert my director and my agent about my ankle. I called the house where I played tennis, hoping the director was still there. He was. I filled him in and said he would have to recast (no pun intended). He thanked me for the information, gave his regrets and immediately began thinking of other actors. He had a film to shoot starting in a few days and this was the fourth of July. I don't know who he finally got. I never went to see the picture. I then called my agent and told him what had occurred. He took it well, I must say. Why shouldn't he? It wasn't his ankle. I must say the loss of a salary was disturbing. Wouldn't it be to anyone?

About three days after I broke my ankle, my agent called and said there was an offer in for me to do a western in Spain. I asked him if he had forgotten that my foot was in a cast. He said the people in Spain would take me, cast and all; and he said he was sending the contract to the house. Sure enough, it arrived. It was some company in Transylvania. (Honest!) The paper of the contract was so thin it was similar to toilet paper. The money was all right, the billing was fine, my ankle wasn't. I couldn't see accepting the job and being able to protect my ankle in a western. The script that followed indicated a lot of riding, walking and running. I knew there was no way. I understood that it was my agent's duty to pass on all legitimate offers. I had to respectfully decline. Later on, I found out who they finally did cast. He was an acquaintance of mine. I heard later that while he was working on the picture, a landrover he was riding in turned over a few times and this actor received a severe back injury.

I did not relish six weeks of inactivity, so after a few weeks, I went to see my doctor. He was also the doctor for the Oakland Raiders, now the L.A. Raiders, so he knew about breaks. He fashioned a sturdy leather-strapped support that I began wearing after four weeks. I could walk, even run, without assistance. No sooner had I received this leather contrivance, when my agent called to say there was a guest-starring role in a series that was shot in Florida. Trivia buff relax—it was *Gentle Ben*. [The episode was called "'Gator Man."] The reason I name it is because there is a story connected with my work there.

I flew down to Florida and began my work. My role was that of a grouchy 'gator-poacher, who befriends the little boy. A lot of the shooting was in the Everglades, where underwater roots and vines were plentiful. I ignored my ankle and plunged in, running through those treacherous, unseen roots. Everything turned out well.

Then one day I was to wrestle an alligator in this water and, by subsequent cuts, drag him up onto the bank and put him to sleep by rubbing his stomach. I was leery of wrestling a six-foot alligator. Everyone assured me it would be safe. (They certainly weren't going to assure me that it wasn't safe.) The alligator's mouth was taped shut by transparent tape. The alligator was rented, so the owner had a rope attached to the alligator's rear leg, so that it could not get away. The alligator was allowed to go into the lake. Once it was some six feet from the bank, I was to go in, wrap my arms around what would be termed its neck and make every effort to get it toward the bank. I went into the water to do my best with the cameras rolling. I grabbed the alligator, and the alligator did what all alligators do: it started what is called the "death roll." It just started rolling over and over and over, and sounding (going down) and rolling. What no one had considered was what happens to the rope the alligator was attached to. It wraps around the alligator and it wraps around me! I became wrapped to the 'gator. He kept spinning and going down. The few times my head broke water, it was to grab a breath. I had no time to call for help. I really thought I'd bought it. I passed out through lack of air. Finally, someone realized my dilemma and pulled at the rope. A few guys went in and got the alligator and me out of the water. It was fully twenty minutes before I regained complete consciousness. We went ahead and finished the scene.

It didn't look like much of a big deal when that series segment was aired. It actually looked tame.

Series star Dennis Weaver remembers Salmi as being a very professional, extremely talented actor. It was obvious to him that he had an extraordinary acting background from New York, where Weaver, too, was a member of the Actors Studio.

Except for almost drowning, supporting his growing family was becoming easier now. He was given roles in numerous films, but it was television that monopolized most of his time. In 1968, however, he was ready for a change of pace. The Broadway stage was calling him back.

While I was in Florida, I got a call from the New York branch of my agency in Los Angeles. The New York agent said there was a job offer.

I'm going to have to backtrack. I was in New York in January of the year before I broke my ankle and I saw my old friend, the producer of *Bus Stop* [Robert Whitehead]. He said he was producing a new play and asked me if I'd like to read it. I was very interested and told him so. It was a new Arthur Miller play [*The Price*]. I read it and liked it very much. The fact that he let me read it meant he was considering me for the play, though he did not say so. He did produce the play and it opened in New York without me. I had read the reviews and they were not good.

I wrote a long letter to the producer, telling him how highly I regarded the play in spite of the reviews, how I considered it a Great American Play, and that in five or ten years, it will be done by some off-Broadway theatre and be rediscovered as the American classic it is. I wrote that Arthur Miller shouldn't have to wait that long. I also wrote that I would like to come to New York and play that role as it should be played.

The main character, Victor, has many deeply-embedded resentments and frustrations that are finally brought out into the open after a lifetime of suppression. Salmi must have identified completely with Victor.

I heard nothing more about it until this telephone call from my New York agent. My agent suggested I take the triangle flight—Florida to New York to L.A.—and asked me to stay in New York for a few days

to work out the contract details for me to step into the role of Victor. It seems the two lead male actors were leaving the play and replacements were in order. I was to play Victor and another actor, now dead, was to play my brother. The other two players in the cast remained.

The negotiations for the contract were funny because the agent was not privy to the past relationship I had with the producer. He thought he was the middle man when, in fact, he became the confused man. My agent called me at my hotel when I got to New York and filled me in on the offer. He told me what salary was offered. I told him exactly how much more I wanted. He said I would blow the deal. I told him to forward my counter-offer. He said he would, and I immediately called the producer and told him what I wanted. It really wasn't that much more. He said okay. My agent called him, he said okay to my agent, my agent called me and said my counter-offer was accepted. I said now that I wanted the billing changed, and he responded with the "you're blowing the deal," again. I called the producer, again my agent called the producer, again my agent called me and said, "It's a deal." Then the dressing room, then other things I can't even remember. By the time the new contract was written, my agent was shaking his head and wondering if he wasn't the best damned agent in the world, or that I was a damned devil.

The actors playing the roles still had a few months to play, so I went back to Los Angeles, script in hand, ready to memorize and ready to trod the Broadway boards again.

By the time I was called back to New York to begin rehearsals for The Price, my ankle had healed and I had memorized the role. I settled myself in New York in the upper West Side, a short cab ride to the theatre. Arthur Miller, himself, was to direct the two new members of the company. This he did magnificently. As we rehearsed on the existing set, Arthur would make notes, copious notes, and at the end of the rehearsal give us our hand-written individual notes. Sometimes he would read them to us before giving them out. He was a great help. He understood the play, naturally, but he didn't know how to get the actor from point "A" to point "C." This was my job and this was the other actor's job. This we did without too much commotion.

One afternoon, the still photographer showed up at the theatre to take pictures to be exhibited out front of the theatre when we, the replacements, took over the roles. When the still photographer showed

The Price. (Photofest)

up, you can imagine my surprise to find that I knew her. She had been the still photographer on a western I had done in Mexico. In fact, she saved the life of Audie Murphy on that film.

Salmi is referring to Inge Morath, who is also Mrs. Arthur Miller. A former swimming champion, she had been looking through her telephoto lens during the filming of *The Unforgiven* when she spotted Murphy (who could not swim because of a bad hip) and his duck-hunting companion clinging to an overturned boat. She promptly dropped everything and swam out to rescue them.

"I thought Albert Salmi was a wonderful actor," says Morath, "but I just never got to know him well. I liked him, he was good to work with."

I think we rehearsed The Price about three weeks, and then we stepped into the roles. The reviewers came out again and the new reviews, though better than the opening reviews, did not give the play the recognition I felt it deserved. I was happy to be doing the

role of Victor, but I was frustrated that the play was not seen as the Great American Play that it was.

The Price ran at the Morosco Theatre from February to November, 1968, then at the 46th Street Theatre through mid-February, 1969. Salmi was playing the lead.

Once, during the New York run of this play, he was very pleasantly surprised to learn that Claire, his girlfriend of the 1950s, was in attendance. Salmi was overjoyed to see her again, and proudly took her from dressing room to dressing room, introducing her to everyone. The visit brought back many happy memories for him.

The actor playing Solomon was Davy Burns, one of the best. He never did a lot of film work, but he worked constantly on Broadway and, pound-for-pound, there wasn't a better actor than him. I adored him.

Back when I was at the American Theatre Wing, I worked at the Alvin Theatre, a legit house, as an usher in the balcony. I worked as an usher for about a year or a year and a half. I saw every performance of every show in that house during that period.

The one show I want to mention was a "Review" with Bette Davis, Davy Burns and others. It opened to good notices. In it there were a lot of blackout comic scenes with Bette Davis and Davy. I saw every performance. Bette Davis was the Hollywood star and personality. Davy Burns was the classic comic and ultimate in the delivery of lines. His method was "the method," but I'm sure he didn't know what "the method" was.

As ushers, we used the stage door to get to a large room where all us ushers changed from our street clothes to the usher's uniform. From there, we went up the aisles to the front of the house, in my case up the stairs to the balcony, to wait for the doors to be opened to allow the audience to come so I could seat them at my station. After the show, we reversed the process—down the stairs, down the aisle, to the big changing room, and out the stage door.

One night, as I was leaving, a notice of rehearsal for the next day was posted on the backstage bulletin board. Bette Davis and Davy Burns were called to rehearsal 4:30 p.m. A good show and they're rehearsing? This, I felt, I must see. So the next day at 12:00 noon, I went in the stage door, through the orchestra, and went up to the balcony and waited. The stage manager arrived first. He turned on a

few stage lights. The work light also was on. Davy Burns arrived, and then Bette Davis. There were, in all, about ten blackout scenes in which these two marvelous people were involved. The stage manager asked Bette and Davy to run through the first scene. As they progressed through the scene, the stage manager would stop them and it was always, "Davy, cut that line," or "change that line to…," or "Miss Davis, you can say this line after this feed from Mr. Burns." This rewriting continued through every scene. I was embarrassed to be a witness to the destruction of Davy's performance and perhaps even the "Review" itself. I felt so sad and so sorry for Davy. Miss Davis and the stage manager left, and Davy sat alone in thought on the stage. He was going over the cuts and changes with a workmanlike attitude, completely lost in concentration on these new developments. It was very close to time for me to change from street clothes to my usher's uniform. I had to pass near the stage to get backstage. When I got near the stage, I said, "Mr. Burns, excuse me for interrupting your thoughts, but you're so great in the show and what happened today is terrible. You're a big star on Broadway. Why do you put up with what was done to you today? You don't have to take it." These aren't the words I used, but the meaning is there. He looked at me for a bit, and then he said, "Someday, my boy, you will know." This is a direct, actual quote. I have never forgotten these words.

Now here I am working in a play with this giant. He was all-professional and never mentioned that meeting. I suspect he never mentioned it because he never coupled this Broadway actor (I had done four Broadway shows at this point) with the Broadway usher who spoke to him some years before. I never mentioned it to him. I'm sorry I didn't, for he spoke to a nobody in a very kind, humorous way.

Rest in peace, Davy.

I understood Arthur Miller and liked him a great deal.

It appears that this professional respect was reciprocated: "I thought him a very methodical actor, who prepared himself for each day's rehearsal and was a very convincing performer in that role," says Miller. "He was both manly and touching."

I haven't mentioned the actress playing my wife, a wonderful Canadian actress, Katie Reid. She also is a marvelous talent. We never had any problems during the whole run of the play. I love her. I think she loves me. So I tell this story with love and knowing that the problem is behind her.

One evening, when the curtain went up, there Victor is discovered on stage. He does a little business for about five or ten minutes and then his wife enters from stage left, crosses Victor, turns to him and speaks her line. On this particular night, Katie entered, crossed, turned and said, "Glah, blah, dalg, crum, glah, bah." I saw that she was absolutely serious, but she wasn't making any sense. I think my line was "I thought the doctor told you not to drink." I said my line, and looked into the wings at the stage manager. Something had to be done. She continued with her nonsensical patter, and I decided to escort her off the stage. As I walked toward her, I could see the curtain coming down. I walked to her and embraced her. As soon as the curtain hit the boards, Katie said, in perfect English, "Aren't you going to act with me?" I was dumbstruck. I couldn't say anything. Katie was taken away to a hospital. She had suffered an alcoholic block. We were told she would be back in about a week.

We had another problem. A paying audience in the house and a missing actress! In this case, we didn't have an understudy. We had a stand-by. That is, we had an actress who was up in the part but, unlike an understudy who would have to be at the theatre at every performance, the stand-by doesn't have to be at the theatre; but he or she must leave a number at which they can be reached. We called the stand-by. I'm sure she went into shock, but she said she'd come soon as possible. This stand-by actress had only rehearsed with the stage manager. We did not know how well she knew the role, if she knew the stage movements, if she could do it. She is Arthur Miller's sister, and I'm sure she never believed she would be called on to play the role. An announcement was made to the audience and they politely waited. The actress finally arrived, she put on her theatrical make-up and got into costume, and we were "off to the races." After "good lucks" all around, we raised the curtain again. There, I was discovered on stage, did my little business, and then came the entrance of my stage wife. She knew the moves, she knew the lines and, though she was tentative, she did well.

When an understudy or stand-by goes on unexpectedly, the stress and tension is transferred to the other actors on stage because you are playing in an unknown, unrehearsed situation. You are determined to protect the play and to protect the new actor by improvisation, by cueing, by anything at hand. The audience must not see a bad performance. Generally, the understudy/stand-by actor comes off well and the other actors seem like blithering idiots. This is probably what happened in that fateful night. We got through the play, the audience enjoyed it—anything out of the ordinary is always appreciated because it is something different. We all were glad it was over. I said to my new stage wife, "See ya' on stage tomorrow."

The next morning, I had no voice. I was absolutely mute; I could produce no sound. I went to a doctor and he told me I had strained and abused my vocal cords to such a degree that I wouldn't be able to speak for a week - coincidentally, the same time Katie Reid would be out. A week of writing notes and no speaking passed and Katie Reid and I returned to the cast. She was no worse for her experience, nor was I. We were back to speed.

While Salmi was working on *The Price* in New York, his family visited, staying with him at the hotel. Their housekeeper, Viola Lepisto, also came along to care for Lizanne and Jenny, as she did whenever their parents were away.

It was during this visit in 1968-69 that the girls finally met their paternal grandmother, Ida, for the first time.

After we had been running about five months, the producer, with Arthur Miller, came backstage one night and got the cast together in my dressing room. The producer said how happy he was with the play as it was now being done. He thanked us individually, then he said that he wanted to take this production to London. Arthur Miller spoke up and said that he would not have considered taking the play to London with the original cast, but he said he would be delighted to have this company perform his play in London. They asked us not to answer immediately, but to think about it because it would be a big move. I knew my answer immediately; it was "yes." I thought that this was the opportunity for the play and, of course, for myself and the other actors. The play would get the recognition it deserved. It was a great play.

All the necessary things had to be done for an extended stay in London—packing and arranging for tickets for the flight. My wife would accompany me. The producer rented a flat for us on Hill Street in Mayfair, so we had a place to put our heads. Neither my wife nor I had been to London before, so it was going to be interesting. We finally got off with a mountain of luggage and arrived in London.

Three cabs took us to 45 Hill. When we got there, we found the flat so small that the luggage filled the bedroom. We slept the first night with my wife on the couch in the living room and me in a chair. My wife, always hysterical, wanted no part of the flat we were in. I called Alex Cohen's office the next day. He came on board as the co-producer, and he was located in London. Alex's office arranged for us to move to 49 Hill Street, a little closer to Hyde Park. Hill Street is located between Hyde Park and Barkley Square. 49 Hill Street flats were larger than those at 45 Hill, but they also were tight. The actor in theatre, unlike feature films or TV, is responsible for his digs. He pays from his pocket for the place in which he stays. We were paying a lot for this flat in London's Beverly Hills, Mayfair.

There are two bits of dialog in *The Price* that seem to illustrate best some parallels between the life of Salmi and his character, in the play:

VICTOR: Not that I'm complaining, but finally there's just no respect for anything but money. You try to stay above it; but you shovel it out the window and it creeps in under the door. It all ends up—she wants. She wants. And I can't blame her for it. Like we've got people in our apartment house, ignorant knuckleheads, they can hardly write their names; but last month a couple knocks on the door to offer us their old refrigerator, buy a new one every couple of years. They know what I make, y'see? And it's that friendly viciousness, just to show who's on top. And things like that are eating her out . . .

SOLOMON: What does she want, a police commissioner? An honest cop is a…is a…(*Struggles for the complimentary term.*)

| VICTOR: | He's a jerk. Took me fourteen years to get the goddam stripes because I wouldn't kiss ass… |

And:

VICTOR:	(*Angered—and his manly leadership is suddenly in front.*) I simply felt it was probably more or less right!
ESTHER:	(*Crossing L. to table, puts cigarette out in ashtray. As a refrain.*) Oh, God, here we go again. All right, throw it away…
SOLOMON:	(*Indicating Victor.*) Please, Esther, he's not throwing nothing away—this man is no fool! (*To Walter, as well.*) Excuse me, but this is not right to do to him![3]

I finally got to the theatre in London's West End, the Duke of York's, one of the most beautiful, intimate theatres I've ever seen. The marquee was up, with the opening date. I went into the darkened theatre and there was the work light! A rehearsal was called for this day. I, as always, was early. I walked around on the stage, spoke out loud from the stage. It all felt good. After a half-hour or so, people started coming in, the actors, Alex, the other producer, Arthur. There we all were, assembled for our artistic assault on London.

In England, the doorknobs are generally set about one foot or so higher than the American doorknob. I noticed that the set builders put the doorknobs English style. I mentioned that, since the play takes place in New York, the knobs should be lowered. The audience should believe in every way that we were in New York and not England. A small thing, but small things add up.

Davy Burns did not come to London. His health would not permit. So we had this jerk playing the Solomon role. Anyone would have been a jerk in the role after Davy's fantastic performance, but this guy was really a jerk. Solomon is written as one of those actor-proof parts. It is so well written that any actor would be good in it. This jerk was not good in it. It became quite evident during the rehearsal period in London before the opening. It's funny that, when an actor is out of his depths in a role, he's either fired or is given special attention by everyone. We all, myself

---

[3] *The Price*, by Arthur Miller. Used with permission from the author.

included, took every opportunity to praise his work. Firing him was out of the question. He had a contract and he was in London.

The cast in London consisted of Albert Salmi, Kate Reid, Harold Gary, and Shepperd Strudwick.

Opening night in London was fantastic. The polite, well-dressed audience, the beautiful theatre, and aura of London, the play we respected and knew so well—everything pointed to success. The curtain came up. Everything went along smoothly, the excitement of playing in front of an English audience was exhilarating. Then came the entrance of Solomon. He entered. The play continued. There was something different about him. I couldn't figure it out as we were playing the scene, and then it came to me. This idiot had put two-inch lifts into his shoes for opening night and told no one about it. When I realized that he had grown to eye level overnight, I became incensed. Victor doesn't like the man Solomon, doesn't trust him, so I used what he had done to my advantage. I never liked him. This night, I hated him. We got through our opening night, the curtain came down, the curtain went up, we took our bows, the curtain came down, and opening night was over. When the final bows were taken and the curtain was lowered, I went over and punched Solomon in the mouth. We were immediately parted. When I explained why I was angry, the other actors said that they had been disturbed by Solomon on stage, but they didn't know why. By throwing us off, or trying to, by this amateurish stunt, he thought his character would shine brightly.

The play was a fantastic hit in London. We never had an empty seat for the run, and there was standing room at every performance. Arthur Miller wrote me a glowing letter, which was my proudest possession.

Charles Marowitz reviewed *The Price* in London in the April, 1969, issue of the English magazine *Plays and Players*. He wrote, "This is a skilfully-woven, faultlessly-structured, well-acted, well-directed piece of work." Marowitz said that no one but Arthur Miller could have written this play. He felt, though, that it did too good a job of explaining the answer to every mystery, making it more a puzzle than a mystery. Nevertheless, he said, "It has been faultlessly directed by the author, and is cast 'in the New York manner' with every type scrupulously chosen. Albert Salmi's perplexed cop is beautifully poised between inarticulateness and insight." It was *The Price* that made London recognize, for the first time, Arthur Miller's talent. "From that time on," Salmi later told *The Spokesman-Review* with pride, "Arthur's been a hot ticket in London."[4]

The play was exhausting for me. I was never off stage and we did the play without an interville (intermission). The play was two hours long. On Broadway, sometimes you would take it easy in a performance, generally on matinee days. In London, I was damned if any audience was going to leave the theatre saying the actor was taking it easy and wasn't working.

When we were there, Pat Neal had had her stroke and was recuperating in her home west of London. (I knew Pat and I had known Roald Dahl in New York, when he had taken a couple of his short stories and fashioned them into a play. Hume Cronyn and Jessica Tandy were the stars of the piece. They played previews in town.) My wife and I went out to their home on a visit one weekend. They were just putting in a covered swimming pool and seemed very happy. It was apparent that Pat was having problems from her stroke. We were out by the pool and Roald told Pat to bring out some tea. My wife offered to help, but Roald said no, Pat would do it. After a while, Pat came out with a tray of tea, but had forgotten the sugar. Roald told her to go fetch it. We finally had our tea and scones, and we settled down for cards, a bridge game. Pat would keep score and no one else, Roald said. All this stuff with Pat and Roald made my wife and me uneasy. Later that evening, Roald explained that he had to keep Pat moving mentally and physically, or she would deteriorate. It was a form of therapy.

Since then, Patricia Neal has made a wonderful recovery. "When he [Albert] and his wife Roberta were in London," she says, "we lived in Great Missenden, Buckinghamshire. We had at least one visit from them. We really adored him.

"Sometime later—I forget how long, I was doing a television film titled, 'Eric', in Stanford. I played the mother of a boy who was dying of leukemia. Albert and his wife had a fabulous house there and they visited me on the set several times and really enjoyed themselves. I also visited them and they treated me magnificently. I really loved it there and they seemed to be getting on so gloriously."

---

[4] *The Spokesman-Review*, "Acting became his life and love", by Beverly Vorpahl (6/17/84).

Salmi discovered that his old friend Robert Sugarman was now living in England as well, so they visited him, too. "I was directing in college theatre," Robert says, "and he told me if I ever did Macbeth anywhere, he would love to play it."

We were fortunate to be in London during the running of the Royal Ascot, and we were determined to go. The man and wife had to get the proper entrance identification that allowed the wearer to get into the Royal Enclosure, which was separate and quite posh. The women had to buy a beautiful outfit, with a cute little parasol. The men went to Moss Brothers to rent a morning coat, trousers and top hat. Also a limousine, with driver, was essential.

At that time, Arthur Nader was in London. He was a writer/producer and he was preparing a show in London. TV, I think. His wife, Adele, agreed to come with us to Royal Ascot. The day came and off we went.

We were boorishly early because we wanted to see everything. Our driver parked the car. He was allowed, as our driver, to come into the enclosure. He had to stand in the back for the whole running. If he left to go to the car or to go anywhere, he could not return. There we were, me in my finest rented livery, my wife and Adele in beautiful dresses, each with their little parasols. We roamed the infield, the paddock, we walked and looked, and there, fifty feet away, was the Queen's box. We went up to the clubhouse and had a glass of champagne. Soon, the enclosure grandstand began filling up and I suggested we pick our seats. It was on a first come, first serve basis. We took three seats on the aisle about ten rows back from the infield. They were nice seats, close to the Queen.

We weren't there long when my wife suggested some finger sandwiches and more champagne. She said she would go up to the clubhouse and fetch it. Adele said she would go along to help. I would watch the seats. They left their little parasols and off they went. Within a few minutes, these two dowagers in full sail swooped down, picked up the two cute parasols, which they deposited in my lap, and they were about to sit down in my wife's and Adele's seats. I fought them tooth and nail. I told them I was a cousin from overseas, as Americans are sometimes called. I told them I was more afraid of my wife than I was of them. They, in turn, pointed to a sign, which said empty seats

cannot be held in the Royal Enclosure. An empty seat can be filled by anyone. No denying these were empty seats, and I was trying hard to preserve them. The two dowagers finally left, shaking their heads and commenting on the rudeness of Americans. I fought off two more couples, begging and pleading, and cousin from over the sea. I went to the point of stretching out and covering all three seats. Finally, here comes my wife and Adele. I was sweating profusely by this time. My wife was carrying a tin tray loaded with finger sandwiches and four glasses of champagne. They explained they had had one at the club-house while they were waiting for the sandwiches. As my wife started to sit, she handed me this tray, whereupon I heard this stately English-man, sitting directly to my left and who had witnessed my battles with the couples who had wanted the empty seats. I heard him say, just loud enough for me to hear, "My Gawd, they're turning the Enclosure into a bloody cafeteria!" My heart sank. I put the tray under my seat and told my wife that I wanted to walk down on the grass of the infield. This I did without further ado. By the time I got to the infield and looked back, there in the seat I only just vacated was this portly En-glish gentleman. I stood for the whole race. We all had a laugh about it afterwards, but at the time it was not funny.

We discovered later that if one wished to go to the clubhouse, or the loo, or wherever, that's where the driver came in. Your driver could come down and sit in your place, to keep it, and then go to the back when you returned—a simple solution to what I thought was an im-possible situation.

We moved, at my wife's insistence, to another, larger flat. It was on Deavery and Hill, just catty-corner from the Dorchester. It was a very large flat and it cost a lot of money. Once a week or so, we would go to Sheppard's Market and stock up on food, as we did a great deal of home cooking. Sheppard's Market was just a grand place, friendly people, just about anything anyone would want, from antiques to doughnuts, which they called "doughies." It was quaint, and just to browse was a delight. I walked many, many times from the flat to the theatre. I always enjoyed walking through Barklay Square. ("...and a mocking bird sang in Barklay Square"—lyrics from a song popular during World War II.) Walking home from the theatre, there was a pub on a side street, just off Barklay Square. If I walked briskly, I would hit the pub at "last call," so I would have my pint and go on home.

About four months into the run, I became run down and exhausted, and went under doctor's care. Twice a week, he gave me Vitamin B shots and something else that, as I remember, made my face rosy red.

On the top of the street the Duke of Yorks was on, the street was St. Martin's Lane. On the top of St. Martin's Lane, just opposite the theatre, where the long-running Mousetrap was playing, was a restaurant frequented by actors, The Ivy. Oh, the after-theatre meals we had in that place! In all the restaurants in all the countries I've eaten in, not one of them ever came close to The Ivy, except maybe Sunday brunch at the Cavanaugh.

In the six months we were there, we haunted the antique markets. [Collecting antiques was Roberta's hobby.] We finally had to purchase a steamer trunk to transport our antique purchases back to America. We bought walking sticks [Salmi's hobby], carved wood pieces, books, oil paintings, knick-knacks, picture frames, clocks. We enjoyed going to Hyde Park for the Sunday concerts. We loved Speaker's Corner, where every subject under the sun was heatedly discussed by anyone and everyone. We also spent some time at the "Les A," a gambling place about three blocks from our flat.

We met Dustin Hoffman with his new wife one evening and ran into an old friend, Roddy McDowall, who was with Ava Gardner. Burton and Taylor stopped for a week at the Dorchester. I, along with Burton and other actors, had a Shakespeare study group years before in New York but, when I called to invite them to the play, they were "busy." Dick Kiley was in town with La Mancha and we met after theatre to shoot the bull and have a few drinks. We both had jackets but no ties. We went to the Ritz and were turned away because we lacked neck wear.

We saw everything in London—the Tower, Westminster Abbey, National Gallery, etc., etc. We went to St. Peter's Cathedral, where the famous whispering corridor or tower is. A whisper will travel hundreds of yards around this circular tower, but to get to the tower one had to climb an open grill spiral stairwell. Going up was easy. My wife has acrophobia, fear of heights. When it was time to go down, she froze, and nothing could get her to move. I pleaded and begged for an hour. I tried to lead her blindfolded, to no avail. Then, miraculously, some English Boy Scouts came by and I don't know how they did it, but they got her down. I think they gave her the old "tight upper lip" routine. I remember I almost was late for curtain because of her fear of heights.

Now it seems it's time to mention the fourth member of the cast. He played the role of my brother in the play. [Shepperd Studwick] He was very workmanlike and unassuming. He did his job, he did it well, he was a professional. I liked him a great deal. He and I went out for a meal after a matinee and, since we weren't very hungry, we stopped at a street vendor and had their fish and chips. We ate at leisure, walked a bit, had a pint at the pub nearby, and went back to the theatre for a "lie down" before the evening performance. My brother enters at the halfway mark of the play and stays to the final curtain. This particular night, everything went fine until about twenty minutes to the end of the play. At this point, my brother dropped out of character, staggered stage left, grabbed a curtain leg (a side panel, which blocks the audience's view of the backstage area), and swung it to and fro. Then he exclaimed rather loudly, "I cannot continue." He clutched his chest and staggered off. My first thought was "heart attack." The stage manager came onstage with the "Is there a doctor in the house?" I rushed off stage and went to his dressing room. Others were there, also. He was lying down with his shirt open, sweating. I don't mean perspiring, I mean sweating. He said it was nothing, but his expression belied his protestations. A doctor was found and we were all ushered from the room to wait outside. After some time, the doctor came out of the room and said that it was nothing serious, just some bad fish. The fish and chips! We went in to see our fellow actor. His sweating had stopped and he had color in his face again. He said he was sorry for the trouble and that he would be ready to resume in a little while. He was true to his word. We lowered the curtain, backed the play up a few pages, took our positions, the curtain went up and we continued where we had left off, but not for long. He again dropped out of character, he again staggered to the curtain leg, he again swung the leg to and fro. (It's funny. I, years ago, saw stripteasers do the same thing at a Burly-Que in Jersey City.) Again he exclaimed, "I cannot continue," and, again, he staggered off. It was like seeing a rerun. His discomfort was real, but his fear that he was having a heart attack was without foundation. He had eaten some bad fish and that was that. He could not be convinced and he did not continue that performance. The audience, however, were still in their seats with no idea of what had actually happened and without any idea of how the play ended.

That bothered Salmi a great deal. According to Peter Roberts' "Green Room" column in the April, 1969, issue of *Plays and Players* magazine, "An obstinate audience sat on till Albert Salmi, who plays the other brother, tried to outline the plot, saying, until Kate Reid who plays his wife in the piece, came to his rescue: 'Gee, I wish you could see this scene—I'm terrible at plot-telling.'" Salmi's first allegiance was to the audience. He did not want them to leave without knowing how the story ended. As it turned out, they got to see it after all.

We played out the rest of the play with the stage manager reading the part of my brother. The audience left, apparently satisfied. Again, anything out of the ordinary is acceptable to an audience, for they love to say, "I was there when this or that happened."

The next day, he was back to normal and he never missed another performance.

As I mentioned earlier, I was exhausted playing this role, and getting more and more so as the months went on.

At the sixth month, my contract expired and I opted not to renew. I wanted to get home. My children were in the care of a nanny in our home in L.A. and six months was a long time to be separated. We packed to go home and all the antiques went into the steamer trunk. I told my wife that we should go through the Chicago customs rather than the New York one. I felt they would be easier on us. We got to Chicago and customs went through our stuff, then I opened the steamer trunk. It took a half-hour for the customs agent to go through the bills of sale and the stuff in the trunk. When he was finished, he said, "That will be fifteen."

"Fifteen hundred?" I asked.

"No. Fifteen dollars."

I paid quickly, locked everything up, called a red cap and got out of there. We had to go from the international terminal to a domestic terminal, and we had a pile of luggage. When we got to the domestic terminal, I gave the red cap twenty dollars and we flew home.

He had missed his children terribly. Salmi had pet names for them: Lizanne was deemed "Sunshine" because of her cheerful disposition, and he called Jenny "Twinkletoes" because she tended to walk on her toes.

Other times, he'd affectionately call them "Pumpkin" or "Princess." Life just didn't seem complete without his little girls around.

Lizanne says, "When Jen and I were growing up, my parents always greeted each other like this: My dad would say 'Morning, Glory', and my mom would say 'Morning, Grouchy Bear.'"

Albert shared his love of literature with his children, reading to them every night before they went to sleep. Among the stories he read them were *Lassie*, *Black Beauty*, *Charlie and the Chocolate Factory*, and *James and the Giant Peach*. (These last two were written by Albert's friend Roald Dahl, husband of Patricia Neal.)

He had a playful side, too, and having kids around gave him a good excuse to indulge it. At night, he would sometimes wrap himself up and do a mummy impression for them. Lizanne says, "We knew it was our dad, and we thought it was quite funny." Having never had a kid sister to tease, the temptation of now living in a house full of females was probably awfully hard for Albert to resist. "He was quite the teaser. He definitely did have a 'little boy' in him that came out rather often!"

Once he was settled back home, Salmi's next project was *The Andersonville Trial* (PBS, 1970). The first day of rehearsal for this drama must have been like a wonderful reunion. He was working once again with Richard Basehart and William Shatner, his brothers in the *The Brothers Karamazov*. John Anderson and Wright King, who had appeared with Albert in a *Twilight Zone* episode, were also members of this cast, as was Cameron Mitchell, with whom he had worked in the *Greatest Heroes of the Bible* mini-series. The director was George C. Scott, whom he had arrested three years earlier in *The Flim-Flam Man*. It was a stellar cast, winning *The Andersonville Trial* both an Emmy and the Peabody Award.

Chapter Five

"You are just bubbling over with the milk of human kindness, aren't you? Driving a nun across the mountain, now you're protecting the honor of the little lady."
— Albert Salmi as Chuck Mathers
The Fugitive, "Angels Travel on Lonely Roads"

Even though Salmi's career was still doing well, life at home had its ups and downs.

Daughter Cas would make visits to their home periodically, but life was not kind to her. Lizanne remembers once when she went with Roberta to pick Cas up for a visit, they looked in the refrigerator and through the cupboards of Peggy Ann's house. There was no food to be found. There *was* a ready supply of alcohol, however. When Roberta told Albert about the deplorable conditions at his ex-wife's house, he realized then that his daughter was not being properly cared for, and felt compelled to do something about it. With Garner's approval, Salmi assumed custody of thirteen-year-old Cas in the fall of 1970.

She welcomed this opportunity to live with her five- and seven-year-old half-sisters, and get to know them better. "I'm really happy now that I'm living with my dad," she wrote to her maternal grandmother. Years later, she would fondly recall sitting in the den, playing gin rummy with her daddy during this time. And his Christmastime Santa act. There would often be birthday parties for the children and, once, a surprise birthday party for Roberta.

The family would often join him in his den and all watch television together—*The Mary Tyler Moore Show, All In the Family, You Bet Your*

Jenny (left), Cas and Lizanne (right). *(Salmi family collection)*

Something Big, 1971. *(Photofest)*

"The Jinx" episode of *Laredo*.

Life, Candid Camera, Truth or Consequences, Name That Tune. He enjoyed watching movies, too, but usually not his own. He liked other people's work—*Blazing Saddles* and *Monty Python and The Holy Grail* were among his favorites.

After a while, however, it became apparent that Cas had become addicted to drugs while living in her mother's house. Salmi was firm with her. He loved his daughter, but he hated her drug addiction, and didn't want his other daughters affected by it.

In August of 1972, Salmi's widowed mother was invited to come from Brooklyn to live with him and his family in Los Angeles. Now his children would have an advantage he hadn't had as a child: They would be able to spend time with and get to know their Finnish grandmother.

Albert Salmi, frequently cast as Mr. Bad Guy. *(Salmi family collection)*

"I remember Ida as being very sweet and not speaking English one hundred percent," says Lizanne. "I remember her saying 'I feel silly,' instead of saying 'I feel chilly.' I thought that was very funny and endearing. I think that she was very proud of her son."

Albert Salmi had his whole family living together with him for the first time—his wife, all three of his children, and his mother.

His work had taken him all over the globe, but home was his very favorite place. Now, it was even better. "Down to earth," is how Jenny describes her dad, whose backyard garden produced a bounty of flowers and vegetables. "He was adorable when he worked in his garden," says Lizanne fondly.

Having arteriosclerosis already, Ida had been with them only nine days when she suffered a cerebral hemorrhage. In a letter written many years later to her other grandmother, Cas describes what happened on that fateful day:

Front row: Jenny, Roberta, and Lizanne.
Back row: Grandma and Cas.

She was lying out on the patio [in a lounge chair] and the maid and I had brought her lunch, and she wouldn't respond, so we knew something wasn't right, so we both carried her inside the house so she could talk to my dad. [We] couldn't speak Finnish (she was born and raised in Finland), so I called my dad [at work] to see what was wrong[5], and he said he would be right home. Meanwhile, we had called the paramedics, which were there by the time Dad arrived.

They rushed Ida to Cedars of Lebanon Hospital, where she hung onto life for three days.

"My dad was really sad when he came home from the hospital," Lizanne says, "and I remember that he didn't want us kids to come to the hospital. He wanted us to remember Ida alive and well."

---

[5] I believe what she meant was that, since Ida couldn't speak English well, Cas was hoping her father could communicate with Ida in Finnish on the phone and find out what the problem was.

Then, on the morning of August 15th, Ida Salmi passed away. His mother's death hit Salmi hard. He silently grieved the loss for weeks.

In the meantime, things weren't working out as well with Cas as he had hoped. At first, she was glad to be there, and all seemed to be going well. Then she ran away from home twice. She was still on drugs in a home that had little tolerance for such things. She appeared to be sabotaging their efforts to give her a good life.

From her perspective, however, it wasn't an ideal environment at all. She wrote a letter to her grandmother eighteen years later that explained what was really going on back then. "When I first went to live with my dad, she [Roberta] said she hated me for being my dad's first born and the only reason I was able to live there was because of him," she wrote. "I was 13 at the time. She made me feel hurt and terrible. She didn't even know me." She said that Roberta would beat Cas and Jenny on the back with a belt, and made Cas eat a snail out of the garden when she misbehaved. When her grades weren't up to Roberta's expectations, she would humiliate Cas by cutting off her hair. She had sent Jenny outside with a sign on her back saying that she was for sale, and locked Jenny and Cas out of the house one night. She would sometimes drop little Jenny off in a strange neighborhood, tell her she wasn't wanted or loved anymore, and leave. "She drug us by the hair a lot and hit us a lot," Cas said. In frustration, the child had blurted out once that she wished she was dead. Her stepmother dared her to prove it by drinking a bottle of rubbing alcohol. Cas began doing just that, but Roberta quickly got an antidote and administered it to her. (Asked if the details of this letter could be exaggerated, Jenny said no—they were indeed true.)

After a while, Cas felt she just had to get away from her stepmother. "I ran away the first time when I was 14, only with the clothes on my back," she said. "My stepmother once again said if she had it her way, I would never have lived there and I was only there because of my dad. I had gone to McClaren Hall [a temporary home for abused children] and at first I refused to go home out of fear, but I did. Well, I come to find Roberta had burned all my creative writings, my school albums, my record albums, everything that meant a lot to me. She also burned TV scripts I had written, which my dad was going to submit for me. She also burned all my clothes." Once Cas was back, Roberta had no choice but to buy her more clothes. "I could only handle it for a short time, so I left again for good [at the age of fifteen], with the clothes on my back. My writings I can never replace or some of the other things which were very sentimental to me. Mental abuse is worse than physical abuse because it

Cas clings to her dad, away from Roberta. *(Salmi family collection)*

goes away eventually, but the mental abuse stays with you forever.

"I had nurse reports from school and neighbor reports, also," Cas wrote. "I tried to take her to court but I lost the case because of their names and money. Roberta actually tried to have me committed to Camarillo State Hospital.

"She turned my dad against me. I warned him over and over again but he never listened. I think he deep down knew what was going on but, for some unknown reason, closed his eyes to it all."

Once Ida died and Cas left, they were back to the original four. *(Salmi family collection)*

These were very serious allegations that Cas was making. Salmi's daughter was still addicted to drugs that were affecting her mind. He was probably unsure whether or not he could even believe her.

"She had him wrapped around her finger and brainwashed him," Cas wrote. She told her grandmother of Roberta's infidelity to her father, and that Salmi knew about it but had always taken his wife back. Indeed, so great was his love for Roberta and his need to have their children near that he would forgive his wife many things over the years.

Nevertheless, the family was now back to the original four. Ida and Cas were both gone, never to return.

Salmi was hired to appear on an episode of *The F.B.I.*, his third guest-starring appearance on this series. Henry Darrow was one of his fellow guest stars in this episode, "Canyon of No Return", and he told *The TV Collector*[6] magazine about the filming of the show.

Darrow said that he and some other cast members were to shoot a scene at the Rogue River in Oregon. Salmi wasn't needed until later in the morning. Instead of sleeping late, however, Salmi was already there when the others arrived at 7:30 a.m. He had brought his fishing equipment, a chair, and his pipe, and was contentedly fly-fishing on this overcast day. Darrow and Salmi had become friends the previous year when they had appeared on an episode of *High Chaparral* together. There was some light banter, then they jokingly assumed phony English accents:

"Aaoohh, did you catch anything?" Darrow asked.

"Yes, I think I've caught a bloody cold!" was Salmi's reply.

---

[6] *The TV Collector*, Jan-Feb. 1994 issue #70 (Order from D. Albert, 6704 Fruit Flower Ave., Las Vegas, NV 89130. e-mail tvc44@concentric.net <mailto:tvc44@concentric.net> . All 112 back issues are still available. Issues #70 and 71 featuring "Petrocelli" are $5 www.angelfire.com/ma/tvcollector/home.html <http://www.angelfire.com/ma/tvcollector/home.html>.)

They would end up working together twice more—on the pilot for a show called *Night Games* in 1974, and in the film *St. Helen's* (1981).

As the years went on, it seemed that Salmi's occupational success caused as many problems as it solved. While he was away working on location, which was happening more often now, life at home had become increasingly troublesome for youngest daughter, Jenny.

"Mom was abusive to me," she says. It wasn't until many years later that she actually told her father how nightmarish life at home had been when he was away; but, the signs of abuse were there all along, even though he may not have recognized them. In early family photos, little Jenny was usually the one standing closest to Salmi, on his other side, away from Roberta. When asked why, she said that she felt protected and safe when her father was near. (Cas had been standing very close to him when she was in family photos, too, probably for the same reason.) "When Dad was getting ready to go away on location, I'd cry and beg him not to go," Jenny said. Albert *had* to go, though. He was the sole support of his family, and working on location was part of his career.

It was probably quite difficult for him to accept that Roberta was anything less than an exemplary mother to his children.

When she was displeased with Albert, Roberta would sometimes threaten to leave him. In September, 1973, she followed through on her threat. She withdrew from the bank the $15,000 that he had inherited, and $11,000 of their community funds, then took the girls with her to a ski resort in Sandpoint, Idaho.

In an apparent effort to give Roberta the freedom that she seemed to want and, at the same time, protect his daughters from harm, Salmi went to his lawyer early in 1974. He wanted to file for divorce. All he asked was a fair division of their property and custody of Lizanne and Jenny.

In response to his initial petition for divorce, Roberta asked the Court for the children, the house, $15,000 attorney's fees, court costs, continued membership in the Racquet Club at Palm Springs, $500 per week in child support, and $2,000 per week in alimony. She also had a restraining order issued against him. Roberta claimed that he had beaten her to such an extent that medical treatment was required, and that he had broken furniture and other objects. She offered little evidence, but because of his bad-guy screen image and her claims of abuse, the Court could very easily believe the worst about him. Roberta was quite likely to win custody, too, due to the amount of

Salmi, Susan Howard and Barry Newman, regulars in the 1974-76 TV series,
Petrocelli. (Photofest)

travel that Albert's work required and the fact that mothers were usually given
custody in those days. So three months after initiating divorce proceedings, he
asked that the case be dropped. She agreed, and the couple reconciled.

Perhaps all he could do to ease Jenny's situation at this point was to
take his family with him as often as possible while he was on location. "I
loved traveling with my parents," says Lizanne. Salmi also spent time with
the girls on weekends, sometimes taking them for trips to the beach or to
the mountains.

Soon after the reconciliation, work began on a brand new NBC television series, *Petrocelli*. Salmi had been the first choice of series creator
Jack Neuman for the role of Pete Ritter, a former policeman who was the
lead character's investigator and right-hand man. He was to co-star as a
regular with Barry Newman and Susan Howard in this show about a New
York attorney who puts down roots in San Remo, Arizona.

"Of the three, Salmi is perhaps the best known to national audiences," said columnist Jack Ryan in *The Dallas Morning News*. "He has
compiled an enviable list of acting credits, but is tagged with one of those
faces everyone knows but can't put together with a name."

On the set of Petrocelli in Tucson, Arizona. *(Salmi family collection)*

Salmi dealt with that phenomenon with good humor. "I'm 'what's his name' when it comes to public recognition. They know they know me but they have trouble putting a name on the face. Maybe it sounds like a rationalization on my part when I claim that I really don't mind not being recognized all the time, but I mean it. As long as they remember the role then I sort of feel it's a tribute to me as a performer." The public might not have known his name, but people in the entertainment industry certainly did.

"You know," Newman later told *The TV Collector* magazine, "this is a business of gossip, and negative gossip, about people…So, before I met Albert Salmi, people had told me to watch out for him."

"So then, of course, I was on guard all the time. After about a month of working with him I realized these stories were all full of crap, you know, he was a terrific guy. I mean, *really*, really a terrific guy!"

Newman was so comfortable with Salmi that he dared to play a practical joke on him. The night before one of Albert's most crucial scenes, Barry had them give him the wrong script to learn, one of the re-writes. The next day, as they started to rehearse, Barry stopped Albert and asked, "What the hell, where are you? What are you talking about? That's not the scene we're doing!" Newman showed him the director's script, which, of course, was different from his. "And Albert was a slow study anyway!

Visiting dad in Arizona when school was out for the summer. *(Salmi family collection)*

So he panicked. He had to go back to the trailer and go over the whole thing. And he was a little angry, but it was fun!" he said.

One thing Newman learned from this was that Salmi took his work much more seriously than he took himself, and the two men remained close friends.

The series was filmed in Tucson, Arizona, and for once, Salmi played none of the stereotypes that he had so often played in the past. He dressed as a modern-day cowboy would in Stetson hat, jeans and boots, but that's where the similarity to his earlier characters ended. In *Petrocelli*, he was the savvy investigator who dug up the facts his attorney-boss needed to win his cases.

Life in Arizona agreed with Albert. Jenny says, "He was born in the wrong era. He should have been a cowboy in the old west." Salmi loved the wide-open spaces in this part of the country, and used this opportunity to do some fishing for bass or catfish. In photographs of him during this period, he appears much happier and more relaxed than he had been earlier. The show filmed for six months each year, six days a week, so Albert was unable to go home on weekends. His role wasn't as demanding as Newman's, however, so he brought his car and spent much of his off-

The girls join their parents for an interview. *(Salmi family collection)*

time exploring the area. "If I didn't get out and roam around and explore," he said to columnist Dick Kleiner, "what would I do? I'd just stay in the hotel, going from my room to the coffee shop and back again. I couldn't do that."

This series not only provided a regular paycheck, but it promoted a happier family life as well. Live-in help would take care of the girls at home while Roberta visited Albert for four or five days at a time during the school year; then the whole family would come to Arizona for the summer.

Lizanne recalls that time in their lives fondly: "When he was filming *Petrocelli*, my mom, sister and I were able to spend two whole summers there with him at the Hilton Hotel. It was really great. My sister and I got our own hotel room, and we each got to invite a friend for a week or so. My dad got a bit upset when he saw the room service and food bill Jen and I ran up at the coffee shop. We ate a lot of watermelon, hamburgers, and French fries. He called us 'the watermelon kids' or 'the French fry kids'. I think that that time was a really great time for my parents, although my mom really hated the really hot weather in Arizona."

Roberta didn't visit the set during this series, Newman says, but, instead, would spend her time playing tennis or at the hotel with the kids and some of her friends who would come visit. Salmi joined his family in the evenings.

Signed to his cousin Helen Hendrickson's son Bruce, during *Petrocelli*. *(Bruce Hendrickson)*

He was happy when his old friend Mark Richman was cast in a guest-starring role once. Their careers had kept them so busy, they had lost touch with each other until now. Of Salmi, Richman says, "He was not a run-of-the-mill guy. He was just an unusual man with a particular kind of speech pattern, and he was a good-natured, warm, open fellow. We drifted apart as life goes on and as our careers varied, then we were reunited again and his new wife came to see us…He invited us to go up to visit him [at their vacation spot in Idaho]." Richman looks back on these times with fondness. "We all adored Albert," he said. "He was like a big teddy bear."

Newman and Salmi would often play tennis or go places together in the evenings after work. "We had a terrific time," Newman says. Salmi never drank on the job, but they would sometimes have a drink when they went out at night. Newman, who was single at the time, said that when they were in town after work, there were plenty of opportunities for Salmi to have been unfaithful to his wife, but he remained loyal.

While in Arizona, Salmi received a welcome letter. He had grown up with his cousin named Helen in New York, but he realized now that he also had another cousin Helen on his mother's side; she lived in Minnesota. He was delighted. "How very nice to hear from you," he happily responded in a letter to Helen Hendrickson. "I honestly did not know I had any living relatives here in the States other than Helen Byron and her children." He brought her up to date on the happenings of his life, gave her his home address and phone number, writing, "Hoping someday to meet you and yours."

Petrocelli was doing well, holding its own in the ratings. When the first season was finished, Salmi went home to be with his family again.

During the 1975 hiatus from the series, he returned to the stage, appearing with Rue McClanahan and John Ritter in Oliver Hailey's *Who's Happy Now?* Ironically, this play was a production of the Mark Taper Forum of Los Angeles (named for Roberta's second husband). The Peabody Award-winning PBS series *Theatre in America* televised the play in May of that year.

Things on the home front were still troublesome, however. Barry Newman tells of a conversation he had had with his buddy that was most disturbing. Albert had told him that, during one of Roberta's fits of anger, she had grabbed a gun kept at their house and taken a shot at her husband. (This incident was mentioned in one of Cas's letters, as well.) It seemed incredible to Barry that Albert was actually laughing about it, but that was the way he handled such things. "He was nuts about her," he says.

Before long, it was time to go back to Arizona for another season of *Petrocelli*. The show was given stiff competition in its second year by ABC's *Starsky & Hutch* in the same time slot. Instead of moving *Petrocelli* to another time or day, however, NBC chose to cancel the series.

"Wow, Dad! Look at all those candles!"
Albert in 1975. *(Salmi family collection)*

Salmi's friendship with Barry Newman lasted the rest of his life, and he would always stop to visit him whenever he was in New York. "He was really a sweetheart of a guy," Newman told *The TV Collector* magazine.

The duration of this series had been a good, happy time in Albert's life. In the second season, he had trimmed down and was looking healthy and fit. As Lizanne tells it, "My dad loved having a series because that meant regular work and a regular paycheck. He really liked his co-stars, too, like Barry Newman. They got along great, and Jen and I really liked him, too."

When filming of *Petrocelli* ended in early 1976, Salmi made a trip to Minnesota. He was asked to present a trophy to the winner of the St. Paul Winter Carnival Ice Fishing Contest. The *St. Paul Pioneer Press*'s outdoor editor, Hank Kehborn, reported that for two hours, six thousand participants vied for first place. Salmi, who had always enjoyed fishing, just couldn't believe this. How could anyone catch a fish in such confusion, he wondered. "This is the darndest thing I have ever seen," he exclaimed. "If anybody had ever told me this, I wouldn't believe it." Most surprising of all was the winner: seven-year-old Daniel Tveit. His catch, a three-pound seven-ounce Northern Pike, was almost as tall as the trophy; and the trophy was almost as tall as Daniel! That wasn't his only prize, either. In addition, the boy received a twelve-foot aluminum fishing boat and six-horse power motor.

When the subject of telemark skiing came up, Salmi told Dave Hill of *The Sun* that he did participate, "but as a spectator, with my wife and my two girls, Jennifer, who's 10, and Elizabeth, who's 12. Make sure you get the ages right. Little girls are very insistent about that. My family comes first—then my work. I work steady and I like my work. That leaves more time to spend with my family. I just don't want to be a star."

He did have one dream regarding his career and family, though. Just once, he would like to have seen his name above the title so he could proudly show it to his children. (Apparently unbeknownst to Albert, his dream had already been fulfilled, although in television, rather than film. Many years before, he received star billing in the *Alfred Hitchcock Presents* episode, "The Jokester.")

Getting back into the routine at home often involved parties of one kind or another. Roberta was very much a "party person," and threw a huge one every year to repay social obligations to as many as one hundred fifty people at a time. At other times throughout the year, they had smaller dinner parties for their closer friends. His naturally-reticent nature put on temporary "hold," Salmi would employ his acting ability in order to appear more sociable for his wife's parties. Sometimes, that took all of his skill. He abhorred phoniness and snobbery, and had a difficult time liking some of Roberta's friends. The social graces did not always come naturally to such a forthright man. Salmi's friend Tim Behrens comments, "He once referred to going out with some of Roberta's friends as an opportunity to 'act' civilized."

Now that the series was over, it took a while for his work calendar to fill up. Nevertheless, Roberta chose this time to have her kitchen remodeled. Parties, a new kitchen, and raising a family all took money, so Salmi uncharacteristically accepted an invitation to appear for a week on a game show. He and Roberta guested together with two other couples on the show *Tattletales*. Because couples' personal characteristics and sometimes-embarrassing anecdotes were often brought to the public's attention on this show, many couples refused to appear on it. The Salmis were good sports, though. During that week's taping, some of their personal traits were, predictably, discussed - among them were Albert's love for his children and compassion for his many lonely bachelor friends. They both agreed that Roberta's criticism was more helpful to him than her praise was.

"I never get praise," he added, to which the audience reacted with the customary "Awwwwwww." Roberta's reasoning was if she didn't tell him what's wrong with his performance, who would? Albert said, "Roberta's my biggest booster."

They also demonstrated their humor. When asked which he would rather visit with Roberta—Paris or a desert island—he mulled it over, then asked, "Has to be with Roberta, huh?" His wife then jokingly mimicked smashing his monitor.

Of the two, they both admitted that she was more money-minded. Roberta explained that Albert just didn't care about money—his interests were more in the areas of art, books, plays, and his various activities.

Salmi and Shamie. *(Salmi family collection)*

Albert with his little girls. *(Salmi family collection)*

When asked which he enjoyed more, getting up in the morning or going to bed at night, she said he liked going to bed at night because it was much more calm and peaceful than the hurry-and-scurry of mornings. Not quite. "You've seen Roberta," he said. "Going to bed!" In his eyes, forty-one year old Roberta was still as beautiful and desirable as ever. She was all smiles for the rest of the show, as any wife would be after an answer like that.

After twelve years of marriage, the Salmis knew each other very well. They were the champs, winning three out of four games that week. (One day had ended in a three-way tie.)

This same year, Salmi was given an award from The Finlandia Foundation, an organization that represented a country dear to his heart, and was presented by its Los Angeles Metropolitan Chapter. Eva Risnel, former President, says, "Every year the Los Angeles Finlandia Foundation...honors some person of Finnish background, either as Finnish-born or American-born. These persons generally have achieved recognition either in the general community or within the local or national Finnish community."

Another former President, Elissa Della Rocca, adds, "The Finlandia Foundation is the most important private source of support for Finnish culture in the United States." The award of 1976 was presented at a "dinner dance honoring Mr. Salmi at the beautiful Los Angeles Music Center ballroom on the top floor," says Eva. "We were pleased to have had the opportunity to meet Mr. Salmi and to let him know that we held him in high regard, for which he was presented with a plaque."

Back at home, things were busy as usual. Roberta had wanted nothing less than the finest education for her children, so they sent them to Westlake, a private school. After school were other activities. Both girls were given piano and guitar lessons, and Lizanne also took English horseback riding lessons at Will Rodgers State Park. "I quit because the horse bucked me off," she says. "My hat [which was similar in construction to a hardhat] fell over my eyes because I fell on my head and, thus, I thought that I was blind until my teacher lifted my hat off my eyes and—voila! I could see!" Lizanne was also given ballet and tennis lessons, spending one summer at Tony Trabert's Tennis Camp in Ojai Valley.

Jenny, on the other hand, had no use for private school. "I hated it," she says. "Thought it was snobby and pretentious."

They had several dogs—black poodles Jezzie and Bonnie, and a lovable shaggy dog named Shamie. For a while they had Pepper, a very skittish dog who was given away when he jumped on Lizanne and bit her on

Grinning at the photographer during the hanging scene of Sweet Creek County War. *(Salmi family collection)*

the cheek. Then there was the lone feline family member, a bluepoint Siamese cat named Tut, who was a permanent member of the family for decades.

For several years, the couple had been taking occasional skiing vacations to Schweitzer Ski Resort, at Sandpoint, Idaho, and, in 1977, they decided to buy a condominium there. Salmi found this part of the country to be such a restful place, quite a contrast from the hurried, complicated life in Los Angeles.

He certainly needed serenity in his life. It seems that Peggy Ann's mother, Virginia, was sending Albert telegrams, insisting that he confirm the claims his wife had made against Peggy Ann when Roberta had tried a few years earlier to have her committed to a mental institution. It's not clear whether or not he was aware of Roberta's attempts, but this was a no-win situation for sure. To give her the confirmation she demanded would make both his wives look bad, but to deny it would be lying, whether he knew it was or not. He chose to avoid Virginia.

Salmi concentrated, instead, on work. In 1977, he was cast in the pilot for a proposed series called *McNamara's Band*. When it didn't sell, they made a second pilot, still with no luck. After spending so much on a condo in Sandpoint, the income from a series would have come in handy. Television and movie offers were coming in, though, and he appeared in the 1976 TV mini-series *Once an Eagle* as a senator, and in no less than five films released in 1977.

The next year, he took Jenny with him to a dude ranch in Wyoming where they were filming *Sweet Creek County War*. "I really enjoyed being with him," she says. It was in such a ranch setting that she felt Albert was most in his element. "He was old-fashioned—a wonderful, wonderful guy." She adds, "He would have been a great cowboy. He was lost in cities. He liked open spaces."

Once they were home again, they got some company. Salmi's cousin Helen Hendrickson took him up on his earlier invitation to visit him that October with her husband Oliver. This was the first time she had seen her cousin in person, so she made sure to bring a camera along.

One month later, on November 8, 1978, Albert was made a "Kentucky Colonel" by Governor Julian M. Carroll of Kentucky. Originating in 1812, this commission is awarded to select individuals. What are the requirements for such an honor? Says the Honorable Order of Kentucky Colonels, Incorporated, "The recipe is no secret formula, simply a blend of friendliness, good fellowship, good will and good fun. Then add the ingredient for a capacity for service and accomplishments in some worthy line of endeavor." Albert Salmi, the Finn from Brooklyn, was now a Kentucky Colonel in good standing.

His excellent work, plus his Finnish origins brought him an invitation to the White House when President Urho Kekkonen of Finland made a state visit to the United States. Salmi was very disappointed that his filming schedule wouldn't allow him to attend, but Roberta went in his place.

Songwriter and poet Stephen John Kalinich was a neighbor of the Salmis during these years in Los Angeles. Of Salmi, he says, "He had a sensitive tenderness to his nature, yet he projected a troubled soul. I would not say we were great buddies, but he embraced me and seemed to enjoy my work. He was a soul in search of something that he never quite grasped, although in his heart he knew kindness and sometimes expressed it. He was in turmoil. You could just feel it. He was always respectful to me, always courteous, and I knew him quite well."

His longtime friend Jack Garfein has insight into the nature of that inner turmoil. Salmi's high ideals led to constant disappointment in both his professional life and his personal life. He would sometimes go into a production, thinking it would be something very important, only to discover that it was just another production in which the bottom line is considered more important than artistic expression. "Now I don't know this about Albert," Garfein said, "but the kind of person who exposes himself that way would have a tendency to become an alcoholic, because they're constantly disappointed. They're constantly heartbroken."

Soon, he was working again with his friend R. G. Armstrong in the movie *Steel*, filmed in Kentucky. They had now worked together in three

Salmi and Sonny Fox, 1981. *(Sonny Fox archives)*

different media—stage (*End As a Man* in 1953), television (a *T.H.E. Cat* episode in 1966), and film. The story revolved around construction of a skyscraper, and they filmed it on the site of the Kincaid Tower, which was being built in Lexington. Salmi and Armstrong would frequently take walks together between scenes. They enjoyed watching the construction of the building and the filming of scenes in which they were not involved. "You become a family on the set," Armstrong said.

Jenny was there during the filming, too, and enjoyed having some time alone with her father, as well. "He and I got along real well," she says. As he took her around to introduce her to his coworkers, he warned Jenny not to get giddy when they got to leading man Lee Majors. She was a typical American girl, though. "I didn't think I would, but I did!" she said.

At the end of filming, an accident occurred that resulted in the death of their stuntman. A. J. Bakunas had been performing a fall from the top of the building when the airbag on which he landed split on impact. Fortunately, Jenny had returned home before that occurred.

Being alone with Dad on location was like a vacation. At home, though, the Salmis were experiencing the same generational problems most American families have. They might have lived in the Brentwood section where many other people of privilege lived, but their home was different. Many of

The 1956 *Bang the Drum Slowly* cast reunites in 1981. Left to right: Sonny Fox,
Rudy Bond, director Daniel Petrie, Sr., George Peppard, and Albert Salmi.
(Sonny Fox archives)

the girls' peers in the neighborhood were given very little discipline or guidance, but Lizanne and Jenny had definite boundaries. With typical adolescent fervor, Lizanne held her ground with Albert when they had a disagreement. "I remember that I wanted to take an existentialist class in high school and he really didn't want me to take it because what he knew of existentialism was all based on *The Brothers Karamazov*," she recalls. "The part he played in the movie left a bad taste in his mouth about existentialism and, considering the part, it is no wonder why. I took the class anyway."

Jenny was the rebellious sort and had had her fill of private school. Like her father, she thoroughly disliked pretentiousness and begged her parents to let her go to public school where the students were more "real." In the eleventh grade, she got her wish.

Salmi's fifty-third birthday on March 11, 1981, was a day of much celebration and love. His two cousins named Helen, Helen Hendrickson and Helen Byron, were there and he was surrounded by family. Soon afterwards, he received a call from his Actors Studio friend Jack Garfein, who was on the west coast to teach a class at the USC. Salmi happily took

With cousins Helen Hendrickson and Helen Byron on his 53rd birthday.
(Helen Hendrickson)

that class. One day, he went up to his teacher and said, "Jack, I want you to know that that experience in *End As a Man* was one of the greatest I ever had. I treasure that experience." Garfein was very moved. Salmi had been in the entertainment industry for many years now, but looked back with longing at the one time in his life that he was allowed artistic purity in his work. Back then, he thought all his work would be like that. Now, he realized how unique the experience was.

One of his next projects was in New York for the filming of *I'm Dancing As Fast As I Can*. Lizanne came along with him and they took advantage of the superb entertainment available. While he simply could not understand the musical taste of the adolescents in his household, Salmi was very much a Gilbert and Sullivan fan. *The Pirates of Penzance* was being performed there, so he and Lizanne went to see it. He enjoyed sharing his interests with his daughters and exposing them to the finer things in life.

Chapter Six

"Don't worry, Preacher. I'm goin' to be around a lot more now."

– Albert Salmi as Albie
Bonanza, "Silent Thunder"

After more than thirty years in the business, things were slowing down for Salmi. He was now fifty-four, and most of the really good parts were going to younger actors. So often the roles he was offered now lacked substance and depth. All they wanted was a certain look, not real acting. This, he felt, was an insult to a true actor. Being in Los Angeles every day only served to constantly remind Albert of the contrast between what used to be and what now was. The pace there was too fast. There was a lot of artificiality. Good, true friendships were rare. Now he wanted real friends, not just acquaintances.

"I'm a laid-back sort," Salmi later told *The Spokesman-Review* reporter. "I hate to travel. I really do."[7]

In 1982, the Salmis decided it was time to consider retirement. They started making their plans to move into their condo in Sandpoint, Idaho.

Part of their attraction to this part of the country was that the lakes and snowy climate of the Great Northwest reminded him of both New York and Finland. He also enjoyed the clean air, the relaxed atmosphere, and the friendly people. There was a genuineness to this part of the country that seemed to be missing in their lives before.

Albert knew that his old friend Gloria Pall was both a fine actress and a licensed real estate agent. Perhaps she could handle the sale of their

---

[7] *The Spokesman-Review*, "Albert Salmi, Broadway's original Bo, sees ghosts at the Civic" (10/8/89)

Relaxing on the set of *Dragonslayer*.
(Salmi family collection)

Brentwood house. He gave her a call. Gloria came to the Salmi home to meet with them. Of this encounter, she says, "They wanted $600,000 something. There was so much bric-a-brac and dozens of photos on the piano as I remember. I told Bobby [Roberta] to box it all up because it was distracting when a buyer walks through. Maybe that's why I didn't get the listing and it didn't sell in the 600 bracket."

Further, she recalls, "He invited me to go with him to the Actor's Studio and Bobby put her foot down and said 'Absolutely not!' So I never went."

Twenty-five-year-old Cas and her father had been keeping in touch by telephone. He could tell that she was letting alcohol and drugs control her life, and no amount of stern, fatherly advice seemed to change this. It was during one of these telephone conversations that he had told her of his plans to move north. Father and daughter then made tentative plans to get together once more before the family left, but Cas never called him back. She was too ashamed to admit to him the personal problems she was having that prevented her from meeting her financial obligations, and her phone had been disconnected. By the time it was hooked up again, it was too late. Albert and Roberta had already gone north.

As for the rest of the family, time had played in their favor: Lizanne and Jenny had matured and Albert had mellowed, so their relationship was much smoother now. The two girls relocated with them.

As Barry Newman had said, Hollywood is a town of negative gossip. In response to the family's move, a rumor was circulating around Los Angeles that Albert went north to receive treatment for cocaine addiction. They couldn't think of any other reason why the Salmis would move away from California and his career. Lizanne, however, assures us that "Dad never had a cocaine habit. He never touched the stuff in his life, as far as I know."

Despite the improved locale, home life hadn't gotten any better for Jenny. Lizanne had left home when she was eighteen, and Salmi was still

The new home in Spokane, 1984.

sometimes away, working on location. Jenny and her mother simply could not get along, so, at age seventeen, she moved out of the family home.

The Sandpoint condo was nice for getaways, but not as a permanent residence. Salmi wasn't ready to be completely retired yet and, atop that mountain, it was isolated and not close enough to an airport to respond quickly when he needed to get to Broadway or Los Angeles; so the couple started checking out the houses in nearby Spokane, Washington. "It's such a beautiful town with beautiful people. I love it," he said of Spokane.[8]

Roberta had definite ideas of what she wanted in a house. While visiting a yard sale there in her perpetual search for interesting antiques, she discovered that a beautiful home on Rockwood in the South Hill section was for sale. Buying it would be highly impractical. It was a huge two-story house—much too large for just two people. This was the house that Roberta wanted, though, so that's the one she got. They bought it in 1984. Spokane then became their primary residence, while they continued to maintain the Sandpoint condo. Because of the tremendous difference in the cost of living of Los Angeles and Spokane, they had $255,000 left over from the sale of the California home, which would help to support them in later years when he wouldn't be working anymore.

By June of that year, fifty-six-year-old Albert Salmi was semi-retired and enjoying a more leisurely pace. This allowed him time for fishing, boating,

[8] *The Spokesman-Review*, "Albert Salmi, Broadway's original Bo, sees ghosts at the Civic" (10/8/89)

Albert Salmi, gardener.
(Salmi family collection)

walking around the neighborhood, and visiting his new friends. "Albert especially enjoyed coming to our lake home and fishing," says one of his best friends, Fred Hanson. "He would sit by the hour on a big rock promontory and cast for fish." Liz Hanson recalls that Albert was very gentle and always wanted to be of help, even with the dishes.

He bought a small boat and kept it in the marina at Bayview, Idaho. All went well until one outing in which he was alone. A storm suddenly occurred, resulting in a very rough trip. Nevertheless, that didn't discourage him from going back out in his boat again at every opportunity.

Some of his happiest times were spent working in his backyard garden. He had learned a secret from the Indians: He would take the fish he caught and use them as fertilizer. It worked. He had a beautiful garden with healthy vegetables, including corn, and robust flowers.

Playing cards was another hobby that Albert was now able to pursue more fully. He also enjoyed chess, tennis, and fencing when willing partners were available.

In the meantime, Roberta started to do the one thing she had been wanting to do—write a book. Albert referred to it as her "Great American Novel."

Beverly Vorpahl, of *The Spokesman-Review*, wrote, "He wears an air of jauntiness. He wears a sporty plaid wool hat on a head of graying hair. He wears a silk kerchief around his neck. Most importantly, he wears a smile that is as friendly as your next-door neighbor's."

"I've gotten everything I wanted out of my career," Salmi told her. "I'm very content. That's why I walked away from it; left it. As you get older, the parts are fewer and farther between, and you start doing parts you don't want to do."[9]

---

[9] *The Spokesman-Review*, "Albert Salmi, Broadway's original Bo, sees ghosts at the Civic" (10/8/89)

He had been quite disap-
pointed, in fact, when he viewed
the finished version of the 1980
film *Caddyshack*. The editing process had cut out all but a few of
his scenes—and in only one of
them was his character a part of
the action.

"Albert and I had a very
pleasant working friendship; I was
a big fan," reporter Beverly says.
"I loved interviewing him; I knew
he'd always provide great fodder
for a story."

He still was asked to appear
in television shows occasionally,
and had quite a bit of TV work
in 1983 because he had aged well
and looked very distinguished.

Albert indulges in his favorite hobby.
(Salmi family collection)

Just the man to play a millionaire, thought the casting directors of *Dallas*
and *Trapper John, M.D.* Still, they continued to put him into bad-guy
roles more often than not.

Many older actors take every opportunity to complain about their lot;
some swear off the industry all together. Not Albert Salmi. He loved acting
and wasn't ready to give it up entirely, so he kept his foot in the door. He
told his agent, Elinor Berger, that he would no longer read or interview for
parts, though—he had already proven himself hundreds of times—but if
they wanted him sight unseen, and the job interested him, he would do it.

A meaningful role was then offered to him in the TV movie *Jesse*,
and they wanted him so badly that no testing or interviews were needed.
This was a gripping story of a practical nurse in Death Valley, on trial
for practicing medicine without a license, even though there was no
doctor available within one hundred miles and she treated patients with
the nearest doctor's long-distance supervision. Salmi's sheriff character
was an integral part of the story, and allowed him to demonstrate the
conflicting feelings that a conscientious sheriff would have when he
wants to uphold the law, but knows that there's sometimes a gray area
with which the law shouldn't tamper. Albert specialized in such com-

With Lee Remick in the 1988 made-for-TV movie, *Jesse*.

plex roles. It provided an opportunity for him to work with Lee Remick again, twenty-eight years after his character gave hers so much grief in the film *Wild River*. This time, their characters were strong allies.

Salmi's acting skills had never been sharper, so his wife arranged yet another project to keep him busy. She had approached Betty Tomlinson, manager of the Spokane Civic Theatre, about the possibility of his teaching some drama classes there. Beginning in 1984, he gave advanced acting classes and directed some one-act plays for them, and at nearby Gonzaga University, as well.

Because his union membership would require him to be paid for acting, Salmi was unable to appear in their plays; but he did whatever else he could for them—never pushing, but just making himself available.

Deane Tomlinson, Betty's husband, says, "He was a credit to the theatre and everyone around him."

"I get a lot of satisfaction out of it," Salmi told *The Spokesman-Review*.[10] He was doing for others what his teachers of long ago had done for him.

Actor/playwright Tim Behrens was one of Albert's students during this time, and worked closely with him for three years, helping him establish his classes at both the Spokane Civic Theatre and Gonzaga University, and also serving as registrar. Behrens considers Salmi his mentor, and is now a full-time actor.

He recalls, "Albert taught downstairs, in what is now called the Firth Chew Studio Theatre, a small (maximum audience is about 140) studio theatre, originally called, appropriately, The Studio Theatre. It has a cement floor, gray, and cement walls, all of which are generally black. The ceiling is rather low—about eleven feet above the floor, so it is difficult to light, but not impossible. As a matter of fact, many of Civic's most moving and modern plays are staged there because it is so intimate.

"Albert stood a great deal when he conversed, but often when looking at the work or commenting on a piece just completed, he would sit either with us in the audience or on a chair just off left of the performing area."

Often, Salmi would serve as a coach of sorts, standing behind the young actor onstage, shadowing him, encouraging him to use his imagination to creatively determine where his character was to go, and how he was to move in a given situation.

"He didn't care about lighting during the pieces," Behrens continues, "so often we just used the work lights or room lights, with no stage

---

[10] *The Spokesman-Review*, "Acting became his life and love", by Beverly Vorpahl (6/17/84).

lighting. Armless wooden chairs (he preferred wooden over metal folding) served as everything from a couch to a bed to a workbench. We would use tables of any ilk, which would become clockmaker's tool bins or blacksmith's anvils or a woman's makeup table.

"Makeup was not used, ever, in class, except when he would talk, specifically, about makeup—but for Albert, makeup was just a skin to serve as an initial beacon of character; the meat was underneath.

"Costumes were different. While mostly they were ignored, Albert made it clear that an actor must participate energetically with the costume designer and director in choice of costume to fit the character. We would occasionally be assigned to go out and work our way from thrift store to thrift store to pick up one or two pieces for a particular scene. He discouraged using just the costume shop at Civic, which was rather vast, because he felt it was important to "get out" with the character inside of you to go costume shopping in the real world.

"Props were the same. Much of the time, we mimed them, as he did when he did his painstakingly detailed scene of the watchmaker. Even though there were no real tools present, we could see each one of them, and we even asked questions about some of the smaller ones we couldn't identify, after he completed the piece. So we were allowed to choose maybe one or, at most, two particular props during a scene—perhaps a vase or a glass of water (that could be anything from poison to champagne) or a cane.

"For the work, the emphasis was on the relationships between the character and the space, and the character and other characters, so these lineaments (costume, prop, furniture) were much less important to Albert than the clear, truthful depiction of the moment of life we played on stage."

Salmi also taught beginning acting classes at Gonzaga University, a Christian/Catholic institution. The setting there was quite a bit different from that of the Spokane Civic Theatre. Behrens describes it: "At Gonzaga University, Albert taught in a much more vast theatre, the Russell Theatre. It can seat, probably, about four hundred, and it is odd in that it used to be a gym or some such thing, so the performing area is down below on ground level, and the first row of the audience closest to the stage is about five feet above it, bleacher-like.

"Albert also occasionally taught in living rooms. It was really unimportant to him about the space; all he wanted was an area that could be cleared and empty, so the actor could take responsibility for filling it in with emotion, substance and truth."

To Salmi, stage work was so much purer, more honest than that of screen and television. He hoped to instill this heartfelt love for the stage in his students. At the Spokane Civic Theatre, he gave two ten-week courses on Saturday mornings, and at Gonzaga University, he gave three. The classes would last all morning. He also taught privately. The sharing of what he had learned from his many years of experience was a boon to anyone fortunate enough to have been his student.

His sense of humor was sometimes apparent in these classes, and he felt an affection for students whose level of dedication matched his own. Normally, he disliked working with amateurs, but these devoted students kept him involved.

Everything he did in class had a purpose. After a student gave a performance or demonstration, Salmi would open the floor up for comments from the other students. Those comments were judged either "valid" or "non-valid" by their teacher. Valid comments were those that were helpful to the actor, giving direction for growth in the art. The students were not to act as theatre critics, he instructed. In this way, he was quite protective of his hard-working students.

For some, gentle encouragement was necessary; to others, harshness worked better, and he was known to be quite sarcastic at times. Praise was given only when it was earned. When the students had done a particularly fine job, he felt a sense of pride in them and invited them for coffee or a drink. That was his way of acknowledging their good work and letting them know it was now time to relax.

While they regarded their teacher with great respect, he was glad when, by the end of the course, they would be calling him "Albert," rather than the stuffy "Mr. Salmi."

Behrens felt that Salmi was the ultimate craftsman of theater arts. He would bring everyone else up to his level. He expected total dedication and commitment from his students. They found that pleasing their teacher involved many hours of hard work, but would be well worth it. He expected such a high degree of single-minded dedication to the craft only because that's what he had always given. "Dad was tough on himself, I think," says Jenny.

It surprised Behrens that his teacher took such risks in his work. This, he had done all his life in many different ways: sledding across Fifth Avenue, using his military leave to go to the forbidden country of Finland, and certainly, showing up for the initial *Bus Stop* audition in plain clothes, rather than Western wear, was chancy, as was not working for five months while the volunteer ensemble perfected *End As a Man* for what they thought would be a single performance at the Actors Studio. Sometimes risks paid off, sometimes they didn't.

Salmi had a great memory and was extremely focused, Behrens feels. Whenever he took on a project, he threw himself into it totally. He wasn't one to do something halfway. When Albert directed one of the plays that Behrens wrote, he did so in a very conscientious way, making staging decisions with great care.

He recommended to his students the book *Respect For Acting*, by Uta Hagen. He loved this book—a book of discussion, philosophy, and practical instruction regarding the acting profession, taking the reader inside the mind of the experienced and dedicated actress who wrote it.

Behrens said that, when one of Salmi's students was playing a character who committed murder, Albert stressed the very enormity of taking a life. Contrary to the casual mindset behind the many killings one sees every day on television, taking someone's life is an extremely significant thing, never to be taken lightly, he told them.

Behrens recalls that during one of the first classes in the series of ten at the Spokane Civic Theatre, Salmi had been teaching his students how to create a believable character and a believable world on stage. When class was over, he invited them to have a drink with him at Cavanaughs Inn at the Park. The students felt honored to be invited. (Behrens says that Albert would have a drink at such times, but he never, ever saw him inebriated.) Salmi excused himself to make a phone call. Right then, he fell to the floor, apparently in tremendous pain and perspiring heavily. It appeared to everyone around him that he was having a heart attack. The students panicked. Some tried to help him while one of them called 9-1-1. Then, just as suddenly, Albert stood back up and went about his business as though nothing had happened. His students were confused. What was that all about?

Actually, he had just accomplished two things: 1) he had demonstrated to his students a first-rate job of purely-believable acting, the likes of which they had never seen before; and 2) he had reassured himself that, now in his senior years and with fewer decent roles being offered to him, he still "had it." Since advanced drama students weren't able to tell that his "heart attack" wasn't real, he knew the talent that had served him so well for so long was still intact and better than ever. His students would remember that lesson on believability for many years to come. Time and again, the man taught by both words and example. "Albert was definitely a showman," Behrens said.

Today, Tim Behrens travels throughout the USA and Canada with his one-man show of the four McManus comedies and corporate McManus programs, having delighted over 200,000 theatergoers in twenty-three states.

"I know that what he [Albert] taught me is on that stage every night, and with me in the dressing room before I go on," he says. "And that is that I put my whole self into it, hold nothing back, and am as truthful with the material and with the audience as I can be. I know he would have appreciated most the fact that I am absolutely exhausted at the end of each performance and have tried not to waver in my concentration and my authenticity."

Deane Tomlinson enjoyed taking fishing trips with Albert. He recalls, too, that Salmi was a frequent casual visitor at the theatre. "You could often see him sitting in the back row of the Theatre, watching a rehearsal or whatever was going on. It was a place to hang out, and conversations could be struck up and friendships made that could last forever," he says.

"Albert was moody," Tim said. Like all actors' lives, his was full of ups and downs. They feel down when there's no work, up when they get a choice role.

In the meantime, Roberta's life was very much up. She was having a marvelous time orchestrating the remodeling of their Spokane house. Once completed, this would be the house of her dreams.

"Albert and Roberta extensively renovated the home, taking the walls down, the studs, exposing plumbing and wiring," says neighbor, Jean Greeley.

Lizanne recalls that the house, built many years earlier, still had some of the original wallpaper and fixtures when her parents bought it. Roberta chose new colors for each room, replacing carpeting and fixtures. She refurnished it completely and, when all was done, "it was totally her. My mom really reveled in decorating. I think that it was a newfound joy for her, and she was quite proud of the finished project."

Bill Carroll was one of the men involved during the renovation. "I met Albert through his wife Roberta, in 1984, when they moved to Spokane, Washington, and bought an old mansion on Rockwood Boulevard. They were in the process of remodeling the house when they needed parts for their dishwasher." After mentioning to Roberta that he was a fan of Salmi's, she invited Carroll to their home to meet him, and perhaps give him some pointers on setting up a woodworking shop in the garage they were building. Albert enjoyed working with his hands, and was hoping to build some benches for their lawn. His agent, however, advised against such a hobby now, since it could cause injury that would prevent him from working. The woodworking shop never materialized.

In the midst of the renovations, the Salmis threw a huge open-house party, inviting so many people that Albert asked Beverly Vorpahl if she thought they should provide valet parking, "or would that appear to be 'over the top'?" They agreed such a luxury would be unnecessary, but the neighborhood was filled with cars on the big day. "They invited half of Spokane," says Beverly. "It was a lovely event, and was certainly the most extravagant affair I ever attended."

"Albert was a very gracious man, showing me all his movie mementos," Carroll reminisces. On display in its holster was a six-shooter that Salmi had carried in a couple of westerns. It had originally belonged to a gunfighter whose first name was Kid. He let Carroll examine it.

Working in all those movies with such famous stars must be so exciting, Carroll thought. It was at first, Salmi told him; but after working for so many years with so many big stars, the novelty wore off. At that point, he had probably "seen it all" and found that regular, everyday people were just as interesting as celebrities.

The two men discovered that they both loved fishing. Several dates were set for them to go out on the boat but, unfortunately, Carroll had to break most of them because of conflicts with work.

"I remember him driving an old, rusted Suburban," says Carroll, "and thinking if I was famous like him, I would be driving a nicer rig; but he used it to get around the fishing areas in Idaho." Actually, Salmi also had a sixteen-year-old Lincoln Continental. A 1980 Cadillac Seville was Roberta's. The family referred to his red and white 1974 Chevy Suburban as "The Beast."

"I think he was a little lonely, moving where he knew few people," Carroll said. "He was a gracious and kind person, and I enjoyed my brief life's encounter with him." Unfortunately, Bill was able to enjoy this friendship for only about a year before he married and moved away.

While Roberta was designing the inside of the house, Albert was using his creative skills on the landscaping. Together, they made this house into a real home, warm and beautiful. They both took great pride in their creation, and held another open-house party to show the completed project to their friends.

Back at Gonzaga University, one of his students broke some heart-breaking news to Salmi. "At the break," says Walt Hefner, "Al and I were having a cup of coffee and I said to him, 'I was sorry to hear that your ex-wife passed away today.' Al momentarily froze and then asked, 'What are you talking about?' I told him 'Peggy Ann Garner, I thought you'd heard.' Al wanted to know how I knew this, and I informed him that it was in the local *Spokesman Review*. It was obvious that Al was very concerned, perhaps shaken, over this untimely bit of information. He informed the Gonzaga class that they were dismissed for the rest of the evening.

"My friend and I walked with Al to the parking lot where he informed us that he didn't feel like going home yet, and would we care to join him at a nearby bar for a drink? My friend excused herself by saying she had to get home. I told Al that I'd meet him there.

"The bar was in a fairly upscale hotel and when we walked in Al wondered aloud if we could find a newspaper there. A paper was available and we sat at the bar and Al re-read the small one column by three inch article a number of times. Finally, he said, 'Poor Cas, now she's all alone. I don't know what I should do.'"

Dear, sweet Peggy Ann had succumbed to pancreatic cancer on October 16, 1984. It seems she had never stopped loving Albert.

After the funeral, Cas discovered that her mother had kept the loving letters that Peggy Ann and Albert had written to each other during the early years of their marriage. She also found diaries that her mother had kept, and realized for the first time what a difficult life she had had. Ever since childhood, Peggy Ann had worn a perky, cheerful mask that belied the pain she was feeling inside. A producer borrowed the letters and Peggy Ann's special Academy Award from Cas, with the promise that he would do a screen tribute to her mother. She never saw them again.

While in California, Salmi was approached by Finnish producer, Markus Selin. They were casting a motion picture, a Finnish-American-English production, in which they wanted him to appear as the United States emissary. The storyline was not particularly good but, once he learned that it would be filmed in Finland, he readily agreed. This would be the opportunity he had been waiting for to revisit his parents' homeland. "…it gives me a chance to jump on my dream to search for my roots," he said. He had met his mother's relatives years earlier, and was now hoping to see them again, and also to get acquainted with his father's side of the family. He and Roberta had planned such a trip in the

Meeting Finnish relatives on the Salmis' trip to Finland in 1984 to film *Born American. (Anne Canta)*

mid-1970s, but those plans had fallen through. Now, at last, it was really happening. Roberta went with him and was introduced to the relatives that her husband hadn't seen since 1947. They were joyously welcomed with open arms and much publicity. Not only was Albert proud to be of Finnish descent, but he was being shown that Finland was quite proud of him, too.

His Finnish heritage had always been an important part of his life. He told the Finnish magazine, *Seura*, "Wherever I'm travelling in the States, Mexico, Spain, around the world, I always have my ears pricked up. If I hear any Finnish spoken, I push myself into the conversation and begin speaking Finnish. That's how I've kept my mother tongue alive all these years. It's also given me a lot of nice friends. We've kept up contact, at least by sending postcards."

Because of this, Albert's Finnish (Tampere dialect) remained very good throughout his life, according to these relatives. It pleased Albert enormously when Finns, in Finland or anywhere else, would approach him after having recognized his name as being of their country. At such times, Albert would immediately switch from English to Finnish, and converse with them in their native tongue. That backfired at least once, though. His friend Robert

Sugarman recalls, "He told me that once a man came backstage and identified himself as Finnish, too. When Al spoke to him in Finnish, the guy was shattered because he didn't know the language."

Roberta had never learned Finnish, but did know one Finnish phrase: "(Mä) rakastan sua," which means "I love you." That was good enough for Albert.

Seura described Albert as "a tall, handsome man, nearly two meters in stature. His hair has become gray with style. A boyish smile appears on his face often. He, if anyone, has the charm of a gentleman."

He was able to get together with some of his relatives at the Hotel Kalastajatorppa in Helsinki for a few hours, and *Seura* was there to record the event. His cousin Paavo Terho told the crowd of the time he saw Albert on TV in the 1958 film, *The Bravados*, in which Albert's character was being dragged behind a galloping horse. Paavo had called to his wife in the kitchen that she should come see this: "I think that relative boy of ours is going to get it this time." Upon hearing this, Albert laughed so hard that tears came to his eyes. "So you still remember it?" he asked. "That and many other tight spots." Now, Salmi informed them, he was working in films and television only enough "to show I'm still around and get enough bucks to keep up my wife." Indeed, it took many, many bucks to maintain the lifestyle to which she was accustomed.

The film he was now doing was entitled *Born American*, and known as *Arctic Heat* outside of the United States. In his first scene, his character arrives at his destination in a very impressive Rolls Royce. How spiffy it would be, he thought, to drive that vehicle around town between scenes! Unfortunately, the car disappeared when the shooting of that scene was over.

The *Seura* reporter observed some of the filming and felt that Salmi was the only actor there who didn't seem to be having any trouble with his role. While the others made mistakes that necessitated retakes, Albert's "gentleman role seems to fit so naturally he doesn't seem to be acting at all." In the filming two days later, however, his character was to reveal his true nature by violently raping a young female prisoner. Producer and writer Markus Selin assured the reporter that that was where the real acting began. He couldn't even imagine Albert really being like that.

When he was not needed on the set, the Salmis were given the royal treatment by their Finnish friends, relatives, and the press. As *Seura* reports, "Albert was taken to a sauna, of course. His visit to the Sauna Society in Vaskiniemi, Helsinki, was memorable. Albert enjoyed the hot sauna but was quite surprised afterward when he was scrubbed by a lady washer, clean as a baby." He remarked good-naturedly, "There I was, lying like a cat on a bed."

Albert particularly relished the Finnish cuisine—just like his mother used to make—and he consequently had to loosen his belt a notch or so. He and Roberta obligingly wore their native Saami ponchos as they took in the culture and sights of this charming country.

After filming was done, they boarded a Finnair plane and headed north to Lapland, where more adventures awaited. A photo in *Seura* shows an intellectual Albert spontaneously performing a Shakespearean soliloquy in the snow.

He even tried riding a sleigh pulled by a very spirited reindeer. It was such a lively ride that he fell off the sleigh, breaking two ribs. He then got up and tried to catch the deer, which veered in another direction and sped off into the horizon.

When the couple visited the Arctic Circle near Rovaniemi, he gamely submitted himself to one of the rituals Laplanders perform for the tourists—"the Lapland baptism." This lighthearted custom involves a bowl full of reindeer milk, magic words and a faceful of the cleanest snow in the world. Both Albert and Roberta were laughing when the photographer recorded this not-so-holy event.

After a busy day, the couple and their escorts rested in the warm Kota. "I've been to many places, but this I could call my home," Albert said contentedly.

A cocktail party was given at Kalastajatorppa in his honor, and many Finnish actors were invited. Journalist Risto Karlsson reported that "Ritva Valkama (a noted, but very down-to-earth actress) was captivated completely by Salmi's charm. Everyone reacted like that. Albert was a wonderful personality. He was quite moved by the party we gave in his honor."

Part of his charm had to have come from the fact that here in Finland, among people very much like those with whom he had grown up in his old Finnish neighborhood, he felt totally accepted and very much at home. Because the Finnish culture was so engrained in him, it was sometimes difficult for Americans to understand his quiet and reserved ways. Here, though, he was one of them—he was among his own people. They understood.

Karlsson says, "I received a sudden call from my home in Lauttasaari. My dog Lulu had been killed. I told this to Albert and Roberta and said I was sorry that I had to leave Albert's party so abruptly. Soon afterwards, I received a telegram: 'As dog-owners, we understand the sadness of your loss. Our deepest condolences, Roberta and Albert.'"

"Travelling can be nice," Salmi told *Seura*, "but you get bored with the life in hotels. After that, the best place is *oma koti kullan kallis*. Isn't that the way it goes in Finnish?" (This means "Own home worthy of gold", which seems to be the Finnish equivalent of the American saying "Home, sweet home".)

Lizanne remembers, "They came home with some interesting, kind of funny-looking hats and some wooden mugs. They sure had a great time in Finland. I think it was one of my dad's favorite trips. He really felt special in his homeland." Indeed, the contrast between Finland, where he had been treated like a king, and America, where the realities of life were sometimes rather harsh, must have been very significant. Perhaps this was the root of the depression that gripped his life a few years later.

Roberta would travel often with Albert when he went on location. Her favorite trip was the one to Egypt, where he was working on the film *Guns and Fury*. She made an indelible impression on Albert's handsome co-star, Peter Graves, who recalls, "Roberta was an absolutely charming girl." Unfortunately, she was riding a horse to the Great Pyramids and the cinch broke, causing her to plummet to the ground and break a couple of ribs. Graves says that Roberta was so miserable with her injury and being taped up that they had to put her on a homebound plane earlier than expected. Still, Lizanne reports, "she said that Egypt felt like home to her. Even though it was a dirty, dusty place, she loved the people and the history." However, "She never got to see the Great Pyramids."

Back in Spokane that May, the Salmis discovered, less than three blocks from their house, the Reverend Dr. and Mrs. Jerald H. Traeger, whom they had met earlier on a plane flight from Southern California to Spokane, had moved in. Dr. Traeger had come to Spokane to serve at Grace Baptist Church and was quite happy to renew his acquaintance with the Salmis. Coffee was always on when he visited them, and Albert would often stop by to see the Traegers during his frequent walks.

The Salmis' next-door neighbors, Dr. and Mrs. Jerry Key, had a tennis court in their back yard, and installed a gate joining their properties so the Salmis could come play on their court whenever they wished. The two couples would often play together, though not in a highly competitive manner—Salmi would frequently play a lighthearted game with his racquet in one hand and a drink in the other.

Whenever possible, he would work in his garden every day. He and his other next-door neighbor, Jean Greeley, would often discuss gardening strategies. "He loved to work in his yard," she said. "We had numerous discussions about his plans for an English garden, and were startled one morning to see him hand-broadcasting seed throughout his yard."

People in the area would comment on his unpretentious qualities and enjoyment of life. His friend Charles Leithe, told *The Spokesman-Review* about a humorous incident they had at a bar: "...the bartender looked at Albert and said, 'You look real familiar. Don't I know you?' And Albert got a great kick out of saying, 'Yeah, I'm from Sandpoint.'"[11]   He didn't feel the need to be thought of here as a Hollywood actor. Instead, he wanted to be just "one of the guys" as he enjoyed the company of regular, everyday people.

On Friday nights, Albert and Roberta would go to Fred and Liz Hanson's house for bridge, dinner, and a lot of laughs. "We really had a good time," Liz says. "It was every Friday night for a couple of years."

"He had a fantastic sense of humor," says Fred. Hanson was in the car business at the time, and Albert, when he was away on location, would sometimes call him up and, in perhaps a German accent, would order seven cars. "He was so convincing!" Sometimes he'd call and say he's from the IRS and was going to audit Fred's taxes, or say he's in Mexico and needs $25,000 bail money. He would really have Fred going for a while, then would begin laughing, which gave him away. They both ended up enjoying the joke.

"Fred and I always do a thing called 'The Cathedral and the Arts'— because we're both Episcopalian—at Christmastime, and both he and Roberta went," says Liz, "and he enjoyed it. He loved it. It happened that night that it was the Spokane Children's Choir, the University Choir, and the Cathedral Choir all singing. He thought it was marvelous."

Salmi had yearned for true friendships, rather than mere acquaintances, and that is what he found in Spokane. The quality of his life was much improved now. He seemed happy, at peace with the world.

Then things slowly began to change. At first, it was subtle.

Salmi was starting to distance himself from the Spokane Civic Theatre, feeling there was no common ground for them. He still had plenty of other things to occupy his time.

---

[11] *The Spokesman-Review*, "Character actor tried to live out of the spotlight", by Tom Sowa (4/25/90).

Finnish cousin Elia Vuorenmaa and Minnesota cousin Helen Hendrickson
pay a visit. *(Helen Hendrickson)*

In March, 1988, Albert and Roberta were visited by his Finnish cousin,
Eila Vuorenmaa and Minnesota cousin, Helen Hendrickson, and they now
remember the Salmi home atmosphere as being warm and peaceful.

Lizanne turned twenty-five six months later, and her father presented
her with a gift of $100 for each year of her life—$2,500. "It was shocking," she recalls, "because my mom said that it was my dad's idea, and it
was something that was slightly out of character."

Albert helped his adopted city publicize the Spokane County Cen-
tennial Celebration by recording one of its public service announcements.
In this video clip, he told the viewers about the talented and forward-
looking pioneers who made the city great. Architect Kirtland Cutter, he
said, designed many of the buildings one hundred years earlier that were
still standing. This spot ran on KREM2 television during the Christmas
season of 1988.

Roles might not have been as numerous or as satisfying for Albert as
he got older, but he was still summoned occasionally for television or

movie work. He was putting on weight now, but it made him an even larger and more menacing-looking bad guy in a 1989 *Young Riders* episode.

He worked with Burt Reynolds in the 1989 film *Breaking In*. The Hansons' daughter was getting married during that time, but Salmi had to remain on location in Portland, Oregon. "Albert called the place where we had the reception," says Fred, "and, of course, congratulated everybody. Then he had Burt Reynolds sing a song to Annie. He was a very sentimental, kind, thoughtful person."

He appeared in a pilot for a dramatic television series that same year, called *B-Men*, as J.B. Slater. If this series sold, it could mean a steady paycheck and his return to the work he loved. It aired on June 27th, but failed to sell.

Then in October of that year, Salmi found himself in Australia for the filming of the *Mission: Impossible* episode, "The Fuhrer's Children." This time, Roberta did not take advantage of the opportunity to travel with him. In this role, he played a power-hungry Nazi supremacist. This was a very distasteful part, more so than most of his bad-guy characters, and was full of racism. The role was about as opposite from his true nature as it could be, but he carried it off in his usual professional manner.

His various roles through the years had to have had an effect on him. Always he influenced the role, but sometimes the role influenced him as well. The story behind this *Mission: Impossible* episode was about brainwashed children. It demonstrated methods used in brainwashing and its negative results. Was Albert starting to see a parallel in his own life?

According to the Australian magazine, *Alpha Control*, Salmi was still quite popular in Australia as Captain Alonzo P. Tucker from two *Lost in Space* episodes, originally aired more than twenty years earlier. When sought out on the *Mission: Impossible* set by *Alpha Control*'s reporter, Salmi was quite friendly, and willing to chat. He elaborated on his fondness for *Lost in Space* and its creator-producer-director-writer, Irwin Allen, on whose other shows he had also guest-starred.

When off the set, however, he mostly kept to himself in his hotel room, except when he and co-star Peter Graves had dinner and a few drinks together. Having worked with him twice before over a thirty-year span, Graves saw something different in him this time. "I could sense more turmoil within him," he notes.

Chapter Seven

"May the Lord lead us from darkness and demons."
– Albert Salmi as Greil
Dragonslayer

By 1990, Albert Salmi had sunk into a deep depression. It had been coming on for quite some time, and was getting progressively worse. Ordinarily friendly, he would now pass friends on the street with only a "hello" before continuing on his way. Gone was his ready sense of humor and the sparkle in his eyes. His whole personality had changed. Frustrations that he had been repressing for years couldn't be held back any longer; and it became quite evident that he was a very troubled man, seemingly carrying the weight of the entire world on his weary shoulders. With acting jobs being fewer now and further between, he no longer had a stage on which to express emotions freely.

He sought refuge in alcohol. Lizanne doesn't think her father was an alcoholic, because his health remained good for most of his life. Also, his drinking did not affect his work or other important things. Until now, he hadn't let it rule his life.

"I think people who are depressed are so deep in a hole that they don't recognize warning signs," she says. Sometimes family members and friends are too close to the situation to see it clearly, though. Rather than realizing their loved one is showing signs of a physical problem, a family member could easily see that person as just being difficult. A gifted actor such as Albert can make it *seem* to disappear when the need arises, but it doesn't really. Depression not only causes a marked change in a person's general

161

mood, but it also alters the way he perceives himself and the world around him. Without professional help, it could take weeks, months, or longer to emerge from the black abyss of despair. Albert did not seek such help.

As if this wretched depression and a lowered income weren't enough of a burden, cancerous growths were now discovered and removed from two different parts of Salmi's body.

Roberta had had all that she could take and now wanted out of their marriage. She also wanted him out of their house. At a time in his life when he needed his wife's love and understanding the most, she was pushing him away. When he needed the comfort of his own home, it was denied to him.

"I know he loved my mom tremendously," said Lizanne.

"Dad was good to Mom," Jenny said, "but she treated him badly."

Salmi had been married only twice in his life, and now he had been rejected by both wives. Roberta let him know that she had already decided who her husband #4 would be. Not only Albert, but their friends, too, felt that she was being quite unrealistic about this man's willingness to marry her.

She had gotten into the habit of walking out whenever she and Albert had an argument. On Sunday, February 4th, they had a quarrel; she left. In the meantime, Albert had time to think. If she was serious about getting a divorce, they had better make some agreement on the division of their assets, he decided. This had been relatively easy to do with Peggy Ann, but it would surely be more complicated with Roberta. He searched for the key to open their antique chest, where they routinely kept $10,000 in cash. He found the key and opened the chest, but the money was gone. He was sure she had taken that money and saw her now as a "thief" who was trying to get more than her half of their assets. He left this note for Roberta to see when she got back home: "I'll meet you at the bank tomorrow to split what's left in the box (less 10,000)." It's a good thing it's Sunday, he noted, so she can't get hold of all their money in the bank, too.

By Monday morning, Roberta had not yet come home, so Salmi went alone to the bank to see what their financial status was. What he learned there utterly shocked him. Throughout their marriage, Roberta had been in complete charge of the family's finances, and he had trusted her. Considering how much he had earned over the years, it seemed that a comfortable retirement was assured. That was not to be, however. He found no savings account. There were no IRAs, stocks, bonds, or cash-value insurance policies. The $130,000 in CDs they had bought about five years earlier was nowhere to be found. They both knew that the money from the CDs were intended to provide what, to Albert, would be a "frugal yet comfortable lifestyle" in their retirement.

"Frugal" was not a word in Roberta's vocabulary, however, and they were now in serious financial trouble. As the CDs matured, she had been cashing them in and supposedly put the money into their safe deposit box. Salmi now discovered that that box had no money in it; the proceeds from the CDs appeared to be completely gone. This meant that Roberta had either spent it all or put it someplace that was inaccessible to him. He suspected the latter, knowing there should have been at least $30,000 to $40,000 left of that money. (His lawyer did discover later that Roberta also had a bank account in her name only.) In addition, five of their checks had been returned due to insufficient funds, and there was a large balance due on their bank charge card. Many thousands of dollars were owed to their creditors, but there was not enough money left to pay them.

Upon learning all this, he was absolutely furious. She had betrayed his trust. Having no money left destroyed his dream of a good retirement. If all their money really *had* been spent, that left only his retirement benefits of $1,057 per month to support them for the rest of their lives. If they lived together, they might be able to survive on that. Split fifty-fifty after payment of their debts, however, it would give them each very little to live on—a dismal situation.

Roberta feared retaliation. Maybe she was expecting his forgiveness once too often. She knew Albert was strong enough to do tremendous damage to a person if he were so inclined; so she hired two private investigators to act together as her bodyguards, and alerted the police that she felt she was in danger. Roberta and her bodyguards were there waiting when he returned home. His financial future was ruined, and now he was face to face with men who had taken the gun that the Salmis kept in the bedroom, removed its bullets, and were now watching him suspiciously as if he were a dangerous criminal. Even though he was very angry, he controlled his temper and remained relatively composed.

Soon afterward, Roberta had an immediate restraining order issued, without a legal hearing, to force him out of their house. She asked that it also prevent him from communicating with her in any way whatsoever, even through a third party. In addition, she bought a miniature Doberman for protection, had a loaded Smith & Wesson J-Model .38 Special on hand, and kept the panic button of the house alarm system with her constantly. When one of her bodyguards wasn't on duty, she would frequently call him to ask what other precautions she should take.

Lizanne and Jenny simply could not understand all this. There was nothing frightening about the Albert they knew. Neighbor Jean Greeley felt the same way: "It was a surprise to us that Roberta expressed concern for her life since Albert seemed to be a gentle person, unlike some of his movie and TV roles." Family friend Felicity Sweeting agrees, adding, "He was a really nice person, loaded with charisma, and even on his 'bad days' he was not an evil person." Sweeting had stayed in the Salmis' home on more than one occasion, and had observed them in both good and bad times.

All of Roberta's precautions seemed not only unnecessary to Salmi, but also expensive. Their liquid assets were quite meager already. These extra expenditures would leave even less for them to live on.

He had moved into a local hotel, Cavanaugh's Inn at the Park, while their condo in Idaho was being leased for the winter. Realizing, however, that the only spending he had any power to control was his own, he soon moved to a cheaper room at Cavanaugh's Value Inn. Even so, his money was running out quickly; so he went to his friend Fred Hanson, who loaned him $5,000 to tide him over until he got back on his feet. Salmi just couldn't believe that Hanson would do that for him. "That's what friends are for," Hanson replied. Salmi was so touched that he sat down and cried. Never are friends more appreciated than when one is feeling rejected and all alone in the world.

In March, the Idaho condo had been vacated, so Salmi then relocated there.

A few days after he had moved out of the house, Roberta discharged the bodyguards. At first, she had been telephoning her lawyer almost every day, but soon discharged him, too, telling him that she wanted to use her attorney-friend in Idaho instead.

Throughout their marriage, having the emotional support and physical presence of his family had been important to Salmi. He had been happiest when working on location when family members were with him. For twenty-six years, when problems arose, he had Roberta to share them with. Together, they had been able to handle anything. They were a team. Now all that emotional support was gone and he was completely alone.

In her affidavit, Roberta had claimed that Salmi became violent when he drank. In his own affidavit, he denied this. He added that both of their daughters were willing to submit affidavits that they had never had any reason to believe he abused Roberta. "My wife's actions over the last several years have been very unpredictable," he stated. "She has treated for the past two years with a psychiatrist, Dr. Woodke, and I am concerned for her mental well-being." Normally, he would have kept such things to himself, but he was citing her history of erratic behavior only because he felt that might explain the reason behind her accusations against him.

He didn't want the divorce, but decided not to fight it. After all, the girls were now grown, so custody was no longer an issue. Back in 1974, Roberta might have been able to get a divorce settlement that would leave him impoverished, but that, too, was now irrelevant. His money was already gone, so he had nothing to lose. All he asked was that the divorce proceed as quickly as possible and their assets, after payment of their essential creditors, be divided equally. He also requested that their two residences be put up for sale immediately. That would give them both money to live on. He told his agent that, once the divorce was final, he planned to move back to Los Angeles and work harder. He seemed to her to be quite enthusiastic about working again.

In an apparent effort to keep depression from completely taking over his life, Salmi tried to use his time productively - he began writing his memoirs. By doing this, he could assess his life and determine what lessons had been learned. Perhaps this would be of help or interest to someone, and might even be a source of much-needed income, if published. Writing these memoirs probably had a therapeutic effect as well.

Roberta was working on her memoirs, too. Having been married to men of prosperity and fame, she knew that she had come into contact with many powerful and world-famous people, and felt that her autobiography would make interesting reading. According to her friend Felicity Sweeting, however, there was more to it than that. Roberta's manuscript was quite explicit, and would be an embarrassment to some very prominent people if it were ever made public.

With a restraining order against him, Salmi was no longer allowed in his own home. Neither could he get any more of the sleeping pills that he and Roberta had been taking for many years, so he went off them cold-turkey when he ran out in March.

Things were coming to a head for the rest of the family, as well. Lizanne felt that her mother simply must be confronted about the way she had treated Jenny all these years. She could never understand why her younger sister had been so terribly mistreated while she wasn't. Lizanne felt her mother had ruined Jenny's life. If Roberta would only acknowledge the abuse and take responsibility for it, things might then begin getting better. It didn't happen. Receiving no satisfaction from this encounter, Lizanne threw an empty Pepsi can at her mother and stormed out of the house.

In the meantime, Salmi's situation was getting worse and worse. Being so far away from Los Angeles, his opportunities to rebuild their savings were limited. Almost everything he had worked for all these years appeared to be gone. Roberta knew where he was emotionally vulnerable and seemed to be using every means she could to hurt him. Why she would continue to intentionally provoke the person she feared was a mystery to their friends. Even though she had the restraining order prevent Albert from contacting her in any way, even through a third party, it was she who would call him. "She would call him up and just be nasty," says Fred Hanson. "She would call him and get him riled up." Even though Roberta could be charming when she wanted to and was very intelligent, Hanson also saw the other side of her. "Roberta was a very controlling person and she could be vicious, vindictive."

The snow had melted in Idaho, and the skiers were gone. On that lonely, isolated mountain, Salmi was separated from his Spokane home and everything he loved - his family, his friends, his work, and his garden. Throughout his adulthood, he had had to make a conscious effort to keep his weight down, but now the pounds were dropping off at an alarming rate. In a month's time, he had lost over thirty pounds. "I think that Dad was very depressed and not thinking correctly," Lizanne said. "It seems to me that he had lost all hope." It was with tears of anguish that he would phone his agent to keep her updated on his whereabouts, just in case a job materialized.

His whole world was falling apart.

Chapter Eight

April, 1990

"That's the way of the world, Trampas. You can only do
what's right and hope people understand."
— Albert Salmi, as Brother Thaddeus
The Virginian, "Brother Thaddeus"

Before depression reared its ugly head, Salmi was a peaceful, content
person. In the Army, he had taken steps to change his assignment from
military policeman to the nonviolent announcer-engineer with the touring entertainers. As a civilian, he had quit his security-guard job because
his employer asked him to carry a gun. Throughout his career, he was
known by his friends and co-stars as a quiet, gentle man. In semi-retire-
ment, he emphasized to his drama students the sanctity of human life.

Prior to his separation from Roberta, he had been on the phone with
Jenny. She couldn't hold it back any longer, and finally told him of the
abuse she had received from her mother for so long. He didn't want to
believe it. Ever loyal to Roberta, he had defended her, saying she would
never do such a thing. Jenny then asked to speak to her mother, so he
passed the phone to her. Roberta denied any wrongdoing.

In retrospect, Jenny says, "Actually, I think he *did* believe me but wasn't
ready at the time that I told him."

Jenny's relationship to her parents was very strained after that. She
hadn't seen or spoken to her father since then. Now, however, her parents

168 Spotlights & Shadows

were divorcing and things between them were different. Now, he was ready to believe.

After staying at their condo for a while, Salmi returned to Spokane and checked into the Jefferson House. He sat down at the desk and worked on his memoirs. He also pulled out his calendar and did some calculations to figure out how to survive on the money he had until the house and condo sold. It wouldn't be easy.

He was spending quite a bit of time with the Hansons now, having dinner with them and just visiting. "There's an auction in Spokane that's a charitable auction called Wampum," says Fred Hanson. "He gave me the pistol and holster that he had used in his movies to give to Wampum to auction off, and Albert was going to go to Wampum with Liz and myself. He was going to get up and give a little spiel about how this was a pistol he used in his movies. He donated it to Wampum."

It seemed to Hanson that things were looking up for Salmi. "He was more concerned about getting things back together and getting himself back on top," he says. "He was talking about doing some more work and that sort of thing." Hanson felt that Salmi was "at a point where he said, 'Hey, it's time to saddle up and get moving.' He was planning on moving ahead."

There was a large cast iron eagle on the Hansons' porch. Time and weather had dulled the colors on it, so Salmi decided he would repaint it for his friends.

Soon after this, he wanted to take his daughters out to dinner, and picked them up at Lizanne's apartment. At this time, Jenny had been on her own for most of the previous seven years and now found herself unemployed, unmarried, and four months pregnant.

"When I saw him again," she said, "he walked into Lizanne's apartment and came up to me. He patted my stomach and said, 'You're really pregnant?' I said, 'Yes.' He asked how I would support the child. I said I didn't know."

This, she feels, must have been the straw that broke the camel's back.

"At dinner," she continued, "he was kind and loving. He seemed sad, yet happy at the same time. I do remember him saying 'I would kill myself but your mother would take all the money.' Lizanne didn't hear it, but I did."

The following Monday, April 23, Lizanne received a large envelope in the mail from her father. Inside was $15,000 in cash and a note that said, "Lizanne, take care of your sister. I love you." She shared the information with Jenny and they both got a very uneasy feeling about it. This had to mean something important but they didn't know what, so Lizanne tried to call her parents. There was no answer.

Salmi had planned to help Fred Hanson open his lake house Saturday, but he never showed up. "When Albert told me he was going to do something, he did it," Hanson says. When he didn't come, Hanson called Salmi's hotel room, but there was no answer. Neighbors had thought that Roberta must be out of town for the weekend since her newspapers weren't being taken inside. She and a lady friend had been planning a two-day vacation at a Seattle spa. Could that be this weekend? A friend went to check on Roberta. When he looked through the window, what he saw was a woman's legs on the kitchen floor. He called the police. Officers forced their way in and found that Roberta was dead of two .25 caliber gunshot wounds to her back. Upon further investigation, they discovered Albert Salmi upstairs in a chair in the office. He, too, was dead, having been shot in the heart at close range with a Colt .45 semi-automatic pistol. The deaths were thought by the coroner to have happened the previous day—he estimated Roberta's time of death to have been Sunday morning, but did not venture a guess as to Salmi's. It was assessed as a murder-suicide, with Albert firing the guns.

Rusty, Roberta's little guard dog, was unharmed. He was found keeping vigil by her body.

It appears that Albert had sacrificed his own life and that of Roberta in order to provide for their daughters and grandchild in the only way he must have thought possible. By seeing to it that Roberta died first, he would know for sure that the girls would then receive his entire estate. If this is so, then it was a father's love, together with the despair and hopelessness of his severe depression, that brought about this tragedy. Also, he might have realized fully now the extent of the abuse his children had received and felt that he had failed to protect them as he should have. The past couldn't be changed, but maybe this would provide a better future for them. Their mother would never hurt them again.

Jenny feels that shooting himself in the heart was Albert's way of symbolizing that his heart was broken. "He had it planned," she says. "He wanted to help me and my child."

Salmi's will would have given everything he had to Roberta if she survived him by thirty days. If she didn't, his assets would then go into the family trust. Roberta was named as the Executor of his estate. This will was originally signed in 1976, and its latest codicil was signed in 1985. Why he didn't simply have a new will drawn up is unknown. Why Roberta, who was known to keep her panic button with her constantly, didn't have it at this particular time is also a mystery.

Jenny feels that her father had planned this just as carefully as he had always done other important things in his life. Roberta's was a quick death, and he timed that large envelope of money to Lizanne to be received when it was too late for her to stop him, because he knew that, had they been aware of his intentions, the girls would have done everything in their power to keep it from happening. He didn't want to take any chances that they would intervene and perhaps accidentally get hurt in the process.

The coroner ran toxicology tests but found no signs of drugs or alcohol in his system. The $15,000 was apparently meant to take care of the girls while the wills were being probated and the residences were being sold.

The police found Albert's Suburban parked in front of the house that the Hansons' had moved from a few weeks earlier, less than a mile away from the Salmi home. The truck had been there since Saturday morning. Behind the front seat was a bag that contained coins and two notes. They said "These coins are worth $500 to a coin dealer. Don't spend them. They may be worth more than $500. Love ya', Dad," and, "Because these coins are all silver and old, they are worth about $500. Don't spend them. Sell them to a coin dealer. Love ya', Dad." Salmi had been very low on money since being banished from his home, but he held on to the valuable coins because he wanted to give them to his daughters.

The fact that Albert made a special effort to see his daughters once more and seemed that evening to be "sad, yet happy at the same time" might be an indication that he had already decided to end his own life. He might have shot himself later that very night had it not been for Jenny's special circumstances. She was going to need a lot of financial help, and that help would have to come from Roberta, but he was not confident that Roberta would provide it.

The purpose of taking the girls to dinner, Jenny feels, "probably was to say good-bye."

There are many things that we'll never know in this life, but one thing of which we *can* be sure is that Albert Salmi was not an evil person. The reaction of his close friends and co-stars to the news of the murder-suicide had been overwhelmingly one of complete shock; the Albert they knew would *never* do such a thing. It appears his purpose was to solve problems. Had he not been suffering from such deep depression, he surely would have come up with better solutions.

Fred Hanson had lost a precious friend that day. "Albert was a very caring, gentle, generous person and my feeling was, as a friend, if there was something I had asked him for and he had the ability, he would have responded. As a friend, he would've done whatever he could. He was just that kind of person. And you know, I saw both sides of it and I saw times when Roberta would be nasty and Albert would just fluff it off. He just wouldn't engage in aggressive behavior. He was a neat person."

To this day, his close friend Barry Newman still can't believe what the newspapers said about him. Albert kill Roberta? That just does not make sense to him. Such a thing, he feels, was not in Salmi's character.

Actor John Saxon agrees. "I was shocked and disheartened when I read the news of Albert and Roberta," he said. Years before, when he had visited their home, the couple would sometimes engage in the sort of bickering banter that one would associate with radio comedies—not the kind of thing that the media was now suggesting.

Petrocelli series creator E. Jack Neuman was among the bewildered. "It was unbelievable, really shocking," he told *The TV Collector* magazine[12], "and Barry and I'll never get over it and neither will Susan."

Seura magazine reported, "The Finnish friends of the famed actor cannot believe it really happened. Salmi, who'd played numerous crooks, was known by his friends as a man with a heart of gold." Indeed, when his friends and costars throughout the world described Albert, the word "gentle" would pop up, over and over again.

After a long silence, producer and writer Markus Selin uttered quietly, "I can't believe it's true. I'm shocked."

Journalist Risto Karlsson shared their disbelief. "In Finland [only five years earlier], Albert and Roberta seemed the happiest of couples. They radiated happiness and tranquility to the people around them. And now, this tragedy comes like out of nowhere!"

"We'll probably never know the truth [regarding the circumstances of his death]," says longtime fan Dennis R. Johnson, "but it's all irrelevant when you speak of Albert's talent and his legacy to us, his fans!"

"How incredibly sad," says television writer S. L. Kotar. "I feel as though I have lost a dear friend."

---

[12] *The TV Collector*, Mar-Apr 1994 issue #71

"I was distressed to hear that in later years, Albert had such unhappiness in his life," says director Dan Petrie, Sr. "For someone of his enormous talent and sweet disposition, the story should have been otherwise."

"He was a good and gentle friend," agrees Robert Sugarman, who, with Salmi, began his career by learning about theatre in New York, then went on to teach acting at college for twenty-five years.

Seura expressed the sentiments of their reporters and readers when it recalled Albert's 1985 visit there: "We were there to see how Albert still loved his relatives in Finland, how he enjoyed every moment in his second home country, like a small child. Everyone who met Albert was fond of him, and this applied also to his wife Roberta."

"Devastating" was how Albert's Finnish relatives described it. Very recently had his cousin Eila visited the couple, and everything had seemed to be going so well then.

Analyzing the psyche of his culture, though, Finnish translator Anders Lustig says, "You know, it seems quite typical to me to keep one's problems to oneself, to ponder them alone and in silence – and then solve them all by a (double) suicide. Finns are not good at showing their emotions."

Most touching of all are the grieving daughters Albert and Roberta left behind. "I miss him and my mother tremendously…I try not to think about that terrible day," says Lizanne.

"Thank God he is finally at peace," Cas wrote to her grandmother, "even though it hurts terribly he had to suffer so many years."

Salmi's friend and neighbor, the Reverend Dr. Jerald Traeger, officiated at his funeral. He offered these words of comfort to the grieving congregation:

"We have met today in respectful memory of a man whom we have known and loved and whom we will ever cherish in tender memory. He added a great deal of happiness and meaning to our lives.

"Albert came to an untimely death in what will always be a mystery to us. In God's own time we will someday know and understand what now is only a vast tangle of hurt and loneliness.

"In Matthew 7:1-2 Jesus, our Savior said, 'Do not judge that you be not judged. For in the same way you judge others you will be judged, and with the same measure you use it will be measured to you.'

"One thing we know, Albert was depressed—he loved Roberta very much, maybe too much, and he could not live without her. Had Albert, because of the overload of pressures and problems and depression, come to a complete physical exhaustion and illness, during which he was not like himself, we would have surrounded him with a double measure of love and understanding. There would have been no condemnation.

"But for Albert, for reasons we do not know or understand, his mind took a direction utterly unpredictable. A direction that was devastating to his own person and disastrous to others.

"In a moment of deep despondency when his reason was held prisoner by paralyzing fear and anger, life ebbed out for Albert Salmi. Only eternal God can know the sickness and suffering which had gripped his mind and spirit. But God does know.

"As for me, I shall always remember him as a very beautiful person. I shall remember the goodness, the kindness and the patience which characterized his life. The rest I can safely leave in the Father's love and mercy.

"I trust that each of you will do the same. Remember the good in Albert's life and the happiness he brought to so many because of his marvelous talent and ability.

"Try to erase from your mind the happenings of these last few days and leave that to God's great love and forgiveness.

"Let us turn to God the Father and to Christ Jesus our Savior for comfort and assurance. When Jesus faced what He knew would be certain death, He said: 'Behold the hour comes, yes, has now come, that you shall be scattered, every one to his own way, and shall leave Me alone: and yet I am not alone for the Father is with Me.' (John 16:32)

"I believe Jesus is saying now to those of you whose shock has turned to bewilderment and grief: 'You are not alone for the Father is with you.' What a difference this assurance made to Jesus in the dark gloom of Gethsemane and when He gave His life on the cross for us.

"And what a difference this assurance can make to each of us today. Hear our Savior's voice as is recorded in John 14:1-4:

'Let not your heart be troubled. Trust in God, trust also in me. In my Father's house are many rooms; if it were not so I would have told you. I am going there to prepare a place for you. I will come back to take you with me that you also may be where I am.'

"Let not your hearts be troubled today. Do not be baffled, distressed beyond comfort, the prisoner of unrelenting grief. Believe in God the Father for you are not alone. This is God's sorrow even more than it is your sorrow. We need not fear if we trust God completely for death cannot end life. God is the God of life.

"A little child in the confusion and perils of traffic in a great city is not afraid as long as he knows his father holds his hand and guides him. So let us, the children of God, grip more firmly the hand of our Heavenly Father for He will lead us safely through the sorrows which beset us. He is not far from any one of us. This God and Father is with you now and forever.

"Your loved one is in His care and keeping, and God is loving, merciful and just. His judgments are just and they are kind for they spring from Fatherly understanding.

"They are not based on partial knowledge and prejudice. They are not the ghostwriters of human indictments and verdicts. They are based on God's full knowledge of all things. Lay hold on the promises of your Father and Savior. Listen to God's voice: 'Fear not for I am with you. Be not dismayed for I am your God: I will strengthen you;…Yes, I will uphold you…when you pass through the waters, I will be with you; and through the rivers, they will not overflow you…for I am the Lord your God, the Holy One of Israel…I am with you.'" (Isa 41:1; 43:2-5)"

– Dr. Jerald Traeger, 1990

Our hearts may be heavy, but Salmi's work lives on. Every now and then, you'll catch him unexpectedly when you're flipping channels; and you'll find yourself putting the remote control down when you see him on the screen, telling you a story, creating yet another character for your benefit. If he's playing a vicious bad guy, he wants us to understand that there really are people like that in the world and we need to beware of them. If he's playing a struggling good guy, he wants us to see that character's virtue and make his inner strength our own.

> "I'm not finished with you yet. I'll be back."
>   – Albert Salmi as Albie
>   *Bonanza*, "Silent Thunder"

Remembering Albert:
His Professional Life

The actor wanted the audience to recognize an unsavory character as truthfully as he could, so that any audience seeing it would be repelled by that individual and vow never to be like him. If one person left a performance saying, "I will never be as bad as that character was", the actor felt fulfilled. If the person left the theatre better than he entered it, we felt we were accomplishing something. The reverse was true, too. If one in the audience saw and believed the goodness in the human condition and sought to emulate this behavior, we, the actors, felt a warm sense of accomplishment…This was better than any …award an actor could get, and still is!

– Albert Salmi
1990

"When we think of character actors, we tend to think of actors that have strong, distinctive personalities, with unique mannerisms that makes them instantly recognizable," says Dave Mazor in his website www.what-a-character.com. "We count on character actors to provide the richness to film and television. We may see the star's name on the marquee, but we all know that the show doesn't go on without the villain…"

Dave Hill, of the St. Paul, Minnesota, newspaper *The Sun*, interviewed Albert in February, 1976. He watched with interest a scenario that had become quite commonplace for Albert. The hostess of the Marquette Inn's Gallery Café asked, "Excuse me, but your face is very familiar. I'm sure I've seen you someplace before."

Everyone knew his face, but not his name, so his family gave Albert a t-shirt bearing his standard reply. *(Salmi family collection)*

Salmi in Minnesota.
(Salmi family collection)

"I'm Albert Salmi," he responded, "if that helps any."

It didn't. The woman continued on her way, wondering why he looked so familiar. Was he perhaps her son's football coach?

As the two men talked over coffee, Albert grinned, "People always remember my face, but they can't put a name to it. I guess that's a compliment, come to think of it." He's probably right. TV viewers and moviegoers were seeing him as his many characters, not as an actor.

"It doesn't bother me because I never wanted that kind of fame," he said. "I've always enjoyed the private life too much to want to be recognized everywhere I go."

Usually the supporting actor, Salmi added much to the films, plays, and television shows in which he appeared. He could be the worst bad guy you had ever seen, making you impatient for the show's hero to give him his comeuppance. On another show, he could be such a heart-tuggingly lovable good guy that you wished for him a happy outcome. One real test of his talent was when he had a role in which his character was both extremes—a bad guy turned good. This, he did extremely well.

Why did they so often cast him as the bad guy or a menacing authority figure? His very size is one reason. He was a powerful and brawny 6'2", and had no problem being as obnoxious as necessary to convince his audience that he was, indeed, that frightening individual. "You only had to look in his eyes to know that there was danger there," says actor Peter Graves, with whom Salmi worked on three projects. "That's one of the things that attracts motion picture producers to certain actors, because they sense a danger there, and they know that an audience will sense a danger and that's what Albert had." He added that Salmi "looked something like Mt. St. Helen's before it blew. You sensed that the volcano was there inside, rumbling."

A truly good actor is practicing what is at once an art, a craft, and a science. The science can be learned in classes, and the craft comes with experience, but the truest art must come from within. As his memoirs show, neither money nor fame motivated him nearly as much as love for the art form itself. He genuinely loved his craft. Being a method actor, he threw himself into his work, body and soul. He took such pride in his profession, in fact, that he wanted to be thought of as "Albert Salmi, Actor." Not star of stage, screen and television - but simply, "Actor."

When it came to his work, Salmi was a stubborn man. He refused to play "the Hollywood game," of wooing those in power or stepping on others in order to get ahead. Instead, he patiently did his job to the best of his ability, giving his audience everything he had to give. He did his work with kindness, never trying to upstage anyone, but, rather, helping his co-stars whenever he could.

Dallas McKennon was a regular with Salmi on the television series, *Daniel Boone*. "I seem to recall one special scene he and I were about to start. Coming back from lunch, I was testing out my scene and I noticed how someone had dropped a tape measure on the floor where Al and I were about to do our shot. Trying to be a good samaritan, I picked it up and started rehearsing the scene with Al. Suddenly, we heard the get-ready call from the assistant, followed by a scream from the camera operator, 'Who the hell moved my floor mark for this shot?' I sheepishly handed it to Al, who declared, 'Somebody must have kicked it during the noon break'. Knowing full well he had saved my neck, that let me know what a truly great guy he was."

Salmi was always willing to teach what he knew to others. "Ninety-percent of acting is reacting," he told *The Spokesman-Review*. "You spend a lot of time listening, reacting to what you're hearing."[13]   A less talented actor in this situation will sometimes appear to be waiting for his co-star to finish her lines so he could say his. Not Salmi. He appears to be taking in every word she says. It didn't matter whether they had done that scene in one take or twenty, each time he reacted as though he was hearing it for the first time. His concentration was total.

His daughter Lizanne says that she remembers his telling her that it was easier for him to play a part that was very unlike himself. "It was also more interesting to play a part that was so different from you, and for that reason, he liked playing colorful and/or bad guys." He did his job so well, in fact, that people often were convinced that he was a real-life brute.

Testimony from people with whom he worked would refute that image. Working with him was a joy, and he was the ultimate professional, they say.

"He was a top class actor," says Peter Graves. "Albert was certainly well-respected by everybody who worked with him and hired him. I knew the first day that I played a scene with him that there was something extraordinary there."

William Shatner stated, "Albert was a wonderful actor and had come from New York as I had, with a great reputation, so it was a privilege to meet him." He was quite pleasant to work with, he says, and "he was a meticulous craftsman."

So exceptional was his work that he was in great demand for shows produced by Quinn-Martin, Irwin Allen, NBC, Paramount, and Twentieth Century-Fox. Each of them would cast him in their projects again and again.

It would be just like Salmi, who worked so painstakingly to develop every movement and nuance of his characters, to have worked out the business in the office scene between his character and that of Julie Newmar in *Twilight Zone*'s 1963 episode, "Of Late, I Think of Cliffordville". The actors' body language was superb as their characters negotiated the plan for him to go back in time to the hometown of his youth. There was an intricate power struggle going on between them, and their movements and gestures told a story that went far beyond the dialogue.

"He was very personable, laughing and joking on the set, yet always serious when the camera rolled. He was a very fine actor," says Stella Stevens, his co-star in the *Bonanza* episode, "Silent Thunder," in which she played

---

[13] *The Spokesman-Review*, "Acting became his life and love," by Beverly Vorpahl (6/17/84).

a young deaf mute. "He got along with Michael Landon very well. They laughed a lot and really seemed to enjoy working together. Albert was a well-respected actor with great professional behavior on the set. I never knew Albert in a social way, but was always proud of the good work we did together."

When some *Bonanza* episodes were released on videotape as *The Best of the 1960 Season*, "Silent Thunder" was among them.

One thing that sticks in Stevens' mind about Salmi was that he appeared to the casual observer to be a simple person, but in reality was quite the opposite. She could tell that he had put much thought into the interpretation of his roles, then performed them so seamlessly that it always appeared to be utterly natural and spontaneous.

"He was a splendid and most interesting actor," stated Jonathan Harris, with whom he first worked in New York City, then again in his two guest appearances on *Lost in Space*.

"He was one of my favourites," says Mark Goddard in a LISA [*Lost in Space, Australia*] interview. "He was an Actor's Studio member, a very dedicated and wonderful actor. So, therefore, he was one of my favourite guests on the show because of the way he worked. He was such a good actor."

Ed Ames, a regular in the *Daniel Boone* series, states that Salmi had a sly sense of humor and was a good, "definitely New York-trained" actor. He was amiable, a nice guy, he says, who got along well with the other performers and crew. The two men would occasionally get together socially, as well.

Russell Johnson, who worked with Albert in the *Twilight Zone* episode, "Execution," remembers most his quietness, which made him refreshingly different. "He was a joy to work with."

Veronica Cartwright, who was also a regular on the *Daniel Boone* television series, agrees: "Albert Salmi was a very witty man, a lot of fun to be around. He said one day as we were doing yet another take with a duck, 'They tell you in the business never to work with children or animals, and look at me. I've got both.' I liked him very much."

Salmi not only good-naturedly did scenes with a duck and a child, but also allowed himself to be regularly upstaged by a goose in that series. As Karen Dusik, the moderator of the Daniel Boone Onelist and webmaster of its site, tells it, "In the first season, it seemed that anytime Yadkin [Albert's character] came to the Boone's cabin, Hannibal [the goose] chased him, honking and hissing, while Yad hollered for help."

Fess Parker, who played the lead in that series, states that Albert's humor was very dry and that he was "pleasantly dour." "The man was a pro," he says.

"Albert was a quiet gentleman and wonderful to work with," says Ruth Buzzi, with whom he appeared on the comedy *That Girl* as her sports-minded boyfriend. "He seemed very secure with himself and his excellent talent. He didn't have to constantly let people know he 'was around' on the set, as many actors do." She went on to say, "Albert, Marlo [Thomas] and Ted [Bessell] were great to work together with and there were tons of laughs. I'm honored to be able to say I worked with Albert."

Some people attribute Albert's quietness to shyness. "Most of my elders I consider self-effacing…feeling they have no business in pushing their face into others," says Finnish-American Allen Salmi, a retired teacher in Michigan. "We felt the Finns in Finland were very similar, but I don't think shyness equals lack of self-esteem."

"Albert was a wonderful actor—generous and, at the same time, quite interior. I remember his great smile and his walk—or swagger," says Nancy Malone, with whom Salmi worked in a 1961 episode of *Naked City*, then again nine years later on *McCloud*. "He had a good humor—we laughed a lot."

Bill Mumy, as young Will Robinson, was in many of Salmi's *Lost in Space* scenes. Bill says, "He was a pleasure to work with and, obviously, one of the most talented guest actors to appear in *Lost in Space*. The two episodes he played Tucker in are two of my favorites. I feel like he and I clicked well together, and he created a very memorable character. I felt bad when 'Will' betrayed him."

"All of the *Lost in Space* cast loved working with him," says Ray Dutczak, "and when I ask them for a favorite, they always mention Albert."

Having worked with Salmi in the late 1960s, playwright and director Arthur Miller admired his work, noting that he could be at once both touching and manly in his portrayals. Miller was also sensitive to the human being inside, and observes, "I had the impression of a very introverted, troubled and affectionate person."

"Albert was a gentle person," says actor R. G. Amstrong, with whom he worked several times throughout his career. "He was a good actor. He did great on Broadway!"

Peter Graves seems to reflect the feelings of many when he says, "He could have been a very big star had a couple more roles come his way that were just right."

Comedian Jack Carter recalls that he worked with Salmi in "The Wrong Way Bus" on a *Dramatic Television CBS Playhouse* presentation. "We became good friends, and always had a big hello for each other when we ran into each other socially or workwise! He was always very private and quiet and different, and always lived someplace away from Hollywood! But he was specially talented so he was entitled to live how he wanted, *a la* Nick Nolte and Mel Gibson." The two men appeared together again on the game show *Tattletales* with their spouses.

Many of Salmi's co-workers had been in multiple projects with him. Dan Petrie Sr., director of the 1956 live broadcast of *Bang the Drum Slowly*, was no exception. Having directed the man several times, he describes Salmi as a "fine actor and dear friend" with an "enormous talent and sweet disposition". He said he "worked easily with his fellow actors" and "had an intuitive grasp on character, finding his was unerringly to the soul of the scene. If he came up with ideas of his own as to how to play the part, he certainly kept them to himself and just plunged in and did them, not talk about them."

Sonny Fox produced the 1981 rebroadcast of the 1956 version of *Bang the Drum Slowly*. The show opened with a present-day interview of some of the people involved in the original production. The first and last excerpts shown were those of Salmi. In that interview, he praised Paul Newman, his co-star, and explained that it was sometimes difficult to create reality on a live stage. "Sometimes it worked; sometimes it didn't," he said, "but you worked very hard to make it work."

Rod Steiger, a longtime friend since their Actors Studio days, was a visitor at their house, as was John Saxon, a fellow Brooklynite. "I did two movies with Albert," John said, "and visited his home in Brentwood on several occasions. We spent several months in Durango, Mexico, working on *The Unforgiven*, and I recall asking Albert's opinion re me and my part. I remember him as open and generous, perhaps self depreciating, in a way."

Sometimes, on-screen, Salmi appeared to be a callous brute, a really obnoxious character. Off-screen, it was a different story. "Albert had to rape [my character]," says Stella Stevens, "and he worked well with the physical handling of me. I remember he was very concerned he might hurt me, and was a perfect gentleman when the rape scenes of his character were over."

In the very first scene of this *Bonanza* episode, Salmi's character Albie sneaked up behind the deaf/mute Annie, who was seated on the ground with a lamb on her lap. He got her attention by shooting the bucket at her feet. It looked very real, and dangerous, perhaps done with camera trickery. Not so. Says Stella, "The gun shot was done just as it looked. It was very hard for me to NOT HEAR the shot, and only react when the lamb jumps out of my lap. At that close range, Albert was an expert marksman. We trusted him."

Salmi was even able to use his size in different ways, depending on the role. It could be seen as an advantage his bully character used to intimidate his adversaries, or as a source of awkwardness to his more humble or self-conscious character.

In American films and television shows, it's customary for the leading man to be the tallest person in the cast, simply because the producers or directors feel that tallness equals power and masculinity in the viewer's mind. Casting directors would be hard-put to find many leading men taller than Albert Salmi, however. What you didn't see on your screen was that sometimes Albert was standing in a hole, or the leading man was elevated somehow when they had a scene together.

There were times, too, that his exceptional physical strength showed, even when it wasn't meant to. Salmi probably did not realize just how strong he was, but it was quite evident to his more observant viewers. In *Silent Thunder*, he had closed the cabin door too hard, causing the rifle beside the door to fall off its wall hooks. Because of Albert's stage training, he just kept right on with the scene as though the falling rifle were part of the storyline; and the mishap stayed in the finished version. As he became more experienced, he learned to moderate the appearance of his strength to better suit his roles. It fit right in with his bully character when, in *Black Oak Conspiracy*, he put his right arm around a resisting woman and easily held her up off the ground. He was 49 at the time.

Even though he could lift a grown man, Lizanne said that her dad never saw himself as being particularly "macho." His view of himself was quite different from the way his fans saw him, which would probably explain why he readily took on roles and accepted camera angles that would be less than flattering to an actor. As Roberta stated on *Tattletales*, there wasn't much ego in him.

Bad guys are necessary in the world of film, though. Without them, good guys wouldn't have much to do. Salmi's bad guys made the good guys look like sterling examples of righteousness. But he was also adept at playing the kind of good guy that evokes sympathy. In *Cloud Dancer*, he rendered a moving portrayal of the gentle, sweet-natured, wheelchair-bound, hero-worshipping brother of the stunt pilot played by David

Carradine. The other characters couldn't walk by Albert's character without lovingly mussing his hair or smoothing it back down.

Even though he was left handed, he had learned to make himself appear right handed when the role called for it. For instance, there were times that handling an object or writing with his left hand would have obscured the audience's view of it. He knew that a gesture is meaningless if the audience doesn't see it.

He was quite a sensitive person, which is a trait that can be very hard on the one who possesses it, but necessary to be a truly great actor. Such a person feels emotions with more intensity than others. That sensitivity served Albert well throughout his career. It enabled him to be aware of human feelings by their mannerisms. Because of this, he was a master of body language. His film *Love Child* demonstrates this quite well. When he, as Captain Ellis, was at last told the truth by the prisoner, he didn't say a word. His body language told it all—he was at first shocked, then glad, then felt admiration for her for having kept her secret for so long.

Which of Albert's many roles had been his favorites? Lizanne lists two plays (*Bus Stop* and *The Price*), one television drama (*Bang the Drum Slowly*), and one movie (*The Brothers Karamazov*). Then she added, "I also think that he liked the character he played in *Lost in Space*." The sparkle in Alonzo P. Tucker's eyes seems to confirm that fact.

Mostly, when asked about his choice roles, Salmi would answer by listing his favorite directors. In that list are Richard Brooks (*The Brothers Karamazov*), Elia Kazan (*Wild River*), and John Huston (*The Unforgiven*). He had been directed by the greatest, and he realized how fortunate he was to have had that experience. Exhausting as it was, the six months that he was playing the lead in *The Price* at the West End in London was the very highest point of his career. "That gave me the most personal satisfaction of anything I've ever done," he told *The Sun*. Because of its artistic purity, his work on *End As a Man* came a close second. It's no coincidence that his two most treasured acting experiences were in plays rather than on screen, because that gave him a rapport with the audience.

"On one occasion Albert and Roberta attended church with us," says neighbor Jean Greeley. "The sermon that morning involved the Bible story of the life of Joseph. Albert proceeded with delight to tell us he had played the part of the jailer in one of his movies on that story of Joseph." (He was, most likely, referring to the *Greatest Heroes of the Bible* miniseries segment entitled "Joseph in Egypt.")

He was always gracious to his fans.
(Photographer: E. Robbins)

Several of his projects have ranked superior in viewers' and critics' opinions. One that is mentioned quite often is the 1962 *Combat!* episode, "Cat and Mouse" in which Albert's Sgt. Jenkins and Vic Morrow's Sgt. Saunders are officers with opposing strategies who are ordered to work together. Sgt. Jenkins sacrifices his life so that Sgt. Saunders can get back alive with the crucial information, only to find that that information was no longer needed. In her book *Combat! A Viewer's Companion to the Classic TV Series*, Jo Davidsmeyer writes: "…I really like this episode. Albert Salmi, as Sgt. Jenkins, is a perfect foil for Morrow's Saunders. It is a pleasure to watch two pros working together under the solid direction of a gifted artist like [Robert] Altman. No false notes in this episode; no gaffs of any kind. When the two sergeants clash, Saunders is up against another Sergeant as equally stubborn, battle-hardened, and certain that 'right' is on his side as Saunders is. Watching this episode, I cannot decide which is the immovable object and which the irresistible force."

She adds, "I greatly admired Mr. Salmi's work. He was a very talented actor." Drawing on his own experience in the military and elsewhere, Salmi was able to put a tremendous amount of realism into his portrayal. In fact, during a scene when his character was giving his name, rank and serial number as his heart was racing, it was his very own Army serial number, with only one digit difference, that he gave.

The Brothers Karamazov was one of Salmi's most memorable films. In a 1996 article about director Richard Brooks, Bob Ross (the *Tampa Tribune* movie critic) wrote, "Not intimated by Dostoyevsky's awesome novel, Brooks turned it into a respectable family tragedy with a strong cast. Lee J. Cobb played the dominant dad. Yul Brynner, Richard Basehart, Albert Salmi and William Shatner (in his screen debut) were his sons."[14]

---

[14] Copyright 1996 *The Tampa Tribune.* Reprinted with permission.

Another well-received role was that of Charlie Rawlins in the 1960 film *The Unforgiven*, in which Albert played the shy suitor of Audrey Hepburn's character, Rachel. In the "Shadows of the Past" website, "Old West Film Favorites" page, this film is listed among the best ever by the voters. Of the twenty-three movies that made this roster in 1999, it's one of only two that also lists the individuals who made up the cast. The host of this website, Floyd D. P. Oydegaard, explains why he considered Salmi an important part of the exceptional cast: "He was a character actor you never forgot. Even though it was strange to see him play a good guy, I accepted any role just as I did his many bad-guy roles, for that was an example of his perfected craft. Whatever role he played always seemed natural. His voice is as clear in my head as his face.

"I just know, as an actor on community stages myself, how talented he was. He seemed to do it so seamlessly and with many a delightful character as well…even his bad guys weren't always too scummy! Just real!"

The Big Valley episode, "Under a Dark Star" is a superb example of Salmi's work. This is a favorite of his fan Constance Isbell. In it, he plays Keeno Nash, a man who had been imprisoned for nine years for a crime he did not commit. The attorney who prosecuted him, after learning of his innocence, is now trying to make amends. The well-meaning lawyer tried to help Keeno integrate back into society, but it was a gentle lady and a puppy who were able to reach him most effectively. From rebellious, resentful, prison-hardened ruffian to accepted, hard-working, happy-at-last employee, he was believable all the way. Television writer S. L. Kotar agrees, "He was born to play that role."

"Salmi represented the heavyweights of Hollywood's troupe of professionals who, to a great extent, are the basis of its success," said Finnish director Olli Alho to *Seura*. "Salmi was not a star himself, but in the U.S., he was a widely-recognized and popular character actor." Alho described Salmi's acting style as rough-cut, but with a certain bear-like sensitivity that Hollywood knew how to use. "It's no wonder Salmi was much appreciated there," he added.

How ironic it was to hear Albert singing "The Streets of Laredo" so menacingly in the 1963 *Rawhide* episode, "Incident of the Pale Rider," as it was that song that had been so prominent seven years earlier in *Bang the Drum Slowly*, in which he played a super-good-guy.

His acting ability over the years did not diminish at all, and he became very distinguished-looking in his fifties. Upon viewing a *Murder, She Wrote* episode filmed when Albert was fifty-six, his longtime fan Chris Barnes commented, "I was amazed how good Mr. Salmi looked. He obviously aged like fine wine."

At first, when asked which of all these roles came the closest to showing Albert Salmi as he truly was, his daughter Lizanne could not think of a single one that did. Upon giving it more thought, she then said that Pete Ritter, the investigator in the series *Petrocelli*, may be the character who was most like her dad. This character was personable, intelligent, resourceful, a team player, and normally mild-mannered, but quite assertive when the situation called for it.

S. L. Kotar and J. E. Gessler, co-authors of one of *Gunsmoke*'s most popular episodes, "Kitty's Love Affair", offer this as a tribute:

"Albert Salmi jumps out of the small screen with one eye half shut, hair askew and a twitch to the lips that could either turn into a menacing scowl or explode into a toothy grin. Gently whispering a line or snarling some words of warning, he spoke with a dialect you could not quite place, but never forgot.

"Albert Salmi was a character actor extraordinaire, equally comfortable as a villain or a downtrodden victim. The two roles, which most exemplify his talent equally, express his diversity.

"In the *Gunsmoke* episode "Mistaken Identity," Mr. Salmi played Ed Carstairs, a wanted man trying to escape the law by assuming another's identity. In one of the most brutal and memorable teasers ever filmed for a *Gunsmoke* episode, Albert's character comes upon seemingly innocuous-looking Mel Gates, who is dying from a rattlesnake bite. As the stricken man begs for help, Carstairs kicks him in the face, then goes through his belongings, before leaving him to die.

"After twenty-five years, this footage stands against any for dramatic impact.

"Perhaps Albert's most outstanding role was as the gentle, reformed river hound, Keno Nash on *The Big Valley* episode, "Under A Dark Star." Wrongly convicted of a crime by then-prosecuting attorney Jarrod Barkley, Keno is released from prison into Jarrod's custody. A regretful Jarrod brings him home to the Barkley ranch, where he is to be trained as a blacksmith. Keno's struggles to reacquaint himself with the world he has been locked away from pit him against a sadistic ranch hand who blames the river hound for the murder of his mother, many years earlier.

"The scenes where Keno describes how he was "born under a dark star," the touching love he develops for a puppy, and the interaction with Nick over animal traps he purposely destroyed immortalize Albert, not only as a great actor, but as someone who always inspired his fellow thespians to reach the epitome of their own talent.

"There was not a time when Albert Salmi's name appeared on a cast list that we did not anticipate a good script and first-rate acting. We cannot ever remember being disappointed.

Summing up Mr. Salmi's career, he made good guest-star roles into memorable episodes and always left the audience shaking their heads and saying, 'No one else could have ever played that role!'"

Afterword

Albert's Family Now

> "Somethin' to look forward to, a mark of achievement…home!"
>
> – Albert Salmi as George Breakworth
> *Sweet Creek County War*

In the Salmi home, Albert was surrounded by females. It might have been difficult for him to express it in words, but his actions proved that his family meant the world to him. From them, he had derived much joy over the years. And it is his much-loved children who are left to carry on.

They miss their parents sorely, particularly at special events in their lives. When Jenny gave birth to their grandson in 1990 and when Lizanne earned her Associate of Arts Degree in 1997, their joy would have been more complete if their parents had been there to share it with them.

Jenny has overcome much in her life. "Something was always wrong with me," she told *The Spokesman-Review*.[15] She wore leg braces for years. Jenny has many of her father's mannerisms and talents. "He was an incredibly sweet, loving man," she says of Albert. "He was a passionate man." The same qualities can be found in Jenny, whose passionate and caring nature is quite evident in her artwork and other projects.

For a while, she followed in her father's dramatic footsteps. Salmi's pull enabled her to get formal training at the Lee Strasberg Studios; then

---

[15] *The Spokesman-Review*, "Salmi's space offering a means of expression for artists and children," by Dan Webster (2/16/95)

191

she used what she learned by starring in a film, *The Ghosting*. The thriller was filmed in Spokane in 1991. "I did it for the money," she says. "It was kind of fun, but I didn't like the plot." Salmi had tried to teach Jenny about acting, but, "I had a hard time learning from my dad because I took the criticism too personally. I felt much more comfortable with an 'outsider'." So, she took lessons in Spokane from one of his students, Tim Behrens. This struck Tim as somewhat ironic, though, because he was teaching Jenny the very same things that Albert had taught him. Acting doesn't interest Jenny nearly as much as writing does, though. She would much rather write scripts.

Her son Judah, who at age nine was the towheaded image of his grandfather as a child, is carrying on the family theatrical tradition, having appeared in some community plays.

Jenny is a talented artist, creating not only paintings, but colorful furniture and ceramics as well. She credits her father for her creativity. Jenny reached out to at-risk young people by using her inheritance to start The Galaxy Gallery in the mid-1990s. The gallery displayed works of art created by these disadvantaged students. "There is so much we can do to make this world a better place," she told *The Spokesman-Review*. The Galaxy Gallery was "an outlet that helps kids feel like they're part of the community. It gives kids a positive way to express themselves."[16] After a while, The Galaxy Gallery had to close its doors due to lack of funding.

Having married at the age of thirty-four, Jenny had been determined to "take her time and do it right." Todd is the man of her dreams, with whom she feels she could spend the rest of her life. While he is in no way a carbon copy of anyone else, Jenny finds that he is very much like her father. Indeed, he is quite tall, light haired, and reserved. In fact, both of his daughters' husbands have much in common with him.

Lizanne inherited Albert's sweet nature and love of gardening. She feels, too, that she has her father's shyness, but her charm and thoughtfulness make this trait barely noticeable. Her concern for others is quite evident in her manner. One thing that is so impressive about Lizanne is her conscientiousness, her sense of responsibility.

She feels that her dad probably influenced her in her decision to work with the broadcast media. She was the receptionist for a television station, also working in its accounting department. She first became in-

---

[16] *The Spokesman-Review*, "Salmi's space offering a means of expression for artists and children," by Dan Webster (2/16/95)

volved with the station when she took a news-writing class in college and found she really enjoyed it. Lizanne enjoyed learning new things about her chosen career, filling in for her co-workers while they took vacations. Gracious and thoughtful, she would make a good representative for any company.

Both girls, like their father, are hard workers. Framed photos of their father can be found throughout both of their homes. They each have cherished memories of him, and his influence continues to this day. Drawing on the strength of their roots and their own resources, Lizanne and Jenny are making the world a better place, each in her own way.

Judah proudly escorts his mother Jenny down the aisle at her wedding, 1999.
(Jennifer LaRue)

As for Cas, she remained something of a mystery to the family for many years. "We haven't seen Cas since we were very young," says Jenny, who is eight years her junior. "The last time we heard from her was soon after Dad's death." There was much going on in Cas' life since they parted. After running away from the Salmi home for good at age fifteen, she eventually went back to her mother's house to live. It seemed the lesser of the two evils at the time, though not by much. At least there wasn't pressure there to give up the addictions she didn't seem to have the will power to overcome.

After her divorce from Albert, Peggy Ann had married a man who did not have Cas' best interests at heart. "Her stepdad introduced her to drugs," her friend Elaine Hill says, "and that is something she never got over."

The environment at her mother's house was obviously not a healthy one, but the only alternative was to be abused by her stepmother. "Cassie could only think about becoming old enough to leave home. She said the minute she was old enough, she was out of there," says Elaine.

Among Cas' maternal grandmother's belongings, discovered in December, 1999, were letters, photos, and documents that, along with Elaine's memories and videotape of Cas, give much information about Albert's firstborn child. If you were to watch the adult Cas from a distance, you would have no doubt who her father was, for she too was tall with blonde hair and blue eyes. Instead of emulating the perfect posture of her mother, Cas had the round-shouldered stance of her father; and she, like he, had to make a conscious effort to keep her weight down.

Other, less visible similarities she had with Albert were her artistic talent, sweet disposition and sensitivity. Her creativity manifested itself in her artwork, stories and poetry. She was also a talented needleworker and, like her dad, enjoyed playing cards and reading.

Cas had a loving relationship with her maternal grandmother, Virginia Garner Swainston. Grandma was always there for her; she was Cas' anchor in the stormy sea of life.

In her search for the love that seemed so elusive, Cas became pregnant at age sixteen. She quit school after completing tenth grade, and gave birth to a little girl on July 17, 1974. She named her Kristie. Unable to provide a home for her, she gave her daughter up for adoption. Eldon and Linda Wilson were delighted to become the baby's new parents and called her Jennifer. The following year, Cas married her child's father, nineteen-year-old Scott Franklin Clark. This union lasted a short time; the couple went their separate ways, apparently never officially divorcing. She learned that her stepmother had used this against her. As she told Virginia, Roberta "convinced my dad that I had married a black man, which really shocked me. The man I married was very white with *blonde* hair and blue eyes."

Even though she had a very strong work ethic, Cas had a difficult time managing her money wisely. She was more inclined to use it to help other people or to finance her addictions than to pay a utility bill, and, consequently, she struggled financially for many years. The jobs she held were almost inevitably ones in which she served others. She worked most often as a waitress-hostess, but also tended bar, cleaned houses, served as receptionist, and took care of a terminally-ill woman, of whom she became especially fond. At age twenty-seven, Cas came to the realization that she, like her mother and grandmother, was alcoholic and sought help for it with Alcoholics Anonymous. She attended their meetings and really enjoyed them, urging Peggy Ann to go,

Cas and her son, Christopher Calvert, 1985. *(Estate of Virginia Garner Swainston)*

too, but to no avail. In spite of her good intentions, though, Cas was unable to control her drinking. She was arrested more than once for drunk driving. Albert would telephone her and sternly advise her to use self-control, to take charge of her life and behave responsibly. He could, so why couldn't she? This was an issue he felt very strongly about. During one of these conversations, Cas became so upset at receiving such criticism from her dad that she hung up on him. She just couldn't handle his disapproval.

Peggy Ann died of pancreatic cancer later that year. After the funeral and cremation, Cas was back in her mother's home and found the diaries that Peggy Ann had kept for many years. Reading through them brought tears to her eyes as she realized for the first time the hardships her mother had suffered in her life. It hurt that they hadn't been able to confide in each other when they needed to so badly.

In November of 1985, Cas had a son with Robert Calvert, named Christopher. Cas felt better able to care for a child now, and wanted to keep Chris. She really tried to be a good mother. She cared very much for her son and dreamed of giving him a stable home life with a sibling to keep him company, but her poor health and many problems kept this from happening. Consequently, Chris' father and paternal grandparents took over his care and have raised him from the time he was a toddler.

Then Cas met John Carl Whiteley, a 6' 2" teddybear of a man who gave her all the love she could ever need. Sixteen years older than Cas, John was the man she had been looking for—a man very much like her father—and she fell in love with him. She marveled at John's patience and simply adored him. Like Albert, John was a blonde-haired, blue-eyed man with a gentle, quiet disposition and a good sense of humor. As the hard-working manager of the KOA campgrounds in Porterville, California, he was the kind of man everyone liked. Elaine reminisces, "We called John 'Big John, The Gentle Giant.'" He loved Cas so much that, Elaine says, "he would literally cry over Cassie and her drugs." John wanted so badly to help Cas overcome them, but nothing he did seemed to work. "There was someone in the campground selling her dope," says Elaine, "and John said if he ever found out who it was, he would kill them."

On May 5, 1988, and September 21, 1992, Cas gave birth to two blonde-haired, blue-eyed daughters. She and John were unable to keep them, however, because social workers were aware of Cas' weakness for drugs and alcohol. Consequently, their babies were taken away to live in more stable homes.

The children Cas had to give up must have weighed heavily on her mind. Elaine Hill recalls, "Terry, the [KOA campground] owner, had a very soft heart, and one time this homeless family came in, and he let them live in their tent, and he also hired the dad to do some work around the campground...They were pitiful. Terry put them in a part of the campground where they would be out of sight of his customers. He just felt sorry for the kids (little girls). One night John could not find Cassie. He looked everywhere, and had decided she was off getting wasted. Now the search was really on, because he wanted to find out who she was buying her drugs from. Well, he found her. She was down at the homeless tent PLAYING with the little girls. She was having a great time. The dirt and the smell didn't seem to bother her. She went down there often, and always took the girls something—a cookie, a candy bar, or even gum. She always had a treat for them." Perhaps Cas was treating those children as she was hoping other people were treating hers. "She was a very sweet and tender woman. She was very soft-spoken."

Cas tried her best to have a positive attitude in her letters to her grandma, but often suffered from profound bouts of depression and attempted suicide once by overdosing on Dalmane. She would isolate her-

Cas, during a visit with her beloved Grandma Garner.
(Estate of Virginia Garner Swainston)

self in their darkened apartment and John would be her only link to the outside world. Then, after about a week, she would suddenly be back outside with her friends, happy again and ready to get on with life. That's when Cas would love to sit around a campfire, singing old rock and roll songs with her friends. She loved to laugh, laughing so hard sometimes that she cried—another trait she shared with Albert.

From a distance, Cas maintained tender feelings for her father throughout the years, feeling sorrow for the sadness that she was sure he was experiencing. She saw Albert as a victim of his wife, and described him as a sweet, kind and naïve man. "I saw my dad on a movie called *Steel* yesterday," she wrote to her grandmother in March, 1982. "He really looks good." Cas yearned to be reunited with him so they could enjoy a good relationship once again, but felt that Roberta was standing between them, determined to keep that from happening. She was sure that her stepmother had not relayed her phone messages and letters to Albert. Cas was mistaken about this. Albert was aware of her efforts, and sometimes did call her; but he was taking a firm stand that she would have to give up drugs in order to be welcome back into the family.

Cas' feelings for Roberta never softened. Not only had she suffered physical and emotional abuse from the woman, but she also felt that Roberta had used and manipulated Albert for selfish purposes. Cas had a hard time dealing with that.

"She loved her father dearly," says Elaine.

Medical records show that Cas was diagnosed with an alcoholic liver, with cirrhosis, in January, 1990. Her health deteriorated from then on, being further complicated by premature heart disease. By June of the same year, she didn't know if life could get any worse. Her beloved father was suddenly gone and Cas now feared losing her grandmother, too. "Grandma," she wrote, "you are all the family I have and I love you very much." Then, as if reassuring herself, she told her, "You'll probably outlive me, anyway."

Cas saw the end coming and wanted to prepare her grandmother for the inevitable, so she had written to her several times about how much she was looking forward to the next life, how much better it would be than her present one. "Souls never die," she wrote. "We will be reunited again when it is meant to be. Remember, there is a reason behind everything, even if we may not understand or see the reason each time...so we must never fear death, yet welcome it with open arms and mind. Try and keep a positive mind and thoughts, because positive energy brings positive results."

Then, on the night of Wednesday, May 17, 1995, at the age of only thirty-eight, Catherine Ann Salmi died. Her addiction to alcohol and drugs had caused cirrhosis of her liver and the hypertensive heart disease that was her official cause of death.

John was devastated. He had tried so hard to protect her from substance abuse, but drugs and alcohol won the battle, and killed his beloved Cassie.

Six months later, after having lost her only child and now her only grandchild as well, Virginia Garner Swainston succumbed to lung cancer on November 5, 1995.

Within two years, John Whiteley, too, was dead. His official cause of death was listed as a heart attack, but it might have been a survivable one. Friends seem to feel that, without his Cassie, he didn't have much will to live. Says Elaine, "I figure that John just grieved himself to death because he honestly loved her."

The Known Works
of Albert Salmi

FILMS

1958   *The Brothers Karamazov* (MGM/Avon)
        aka: *The Murderer Dmitri Karamazov*
        The Bravados (Twentieth Century-Fox)

1960   *The Unforgiven* (James Productions)
        Wild River (Twentieth Century-Fox)

1964   *Outrage* (MGM/Martin Ritt/Kayos/KHF/Harvest/
        February)
        aka: *Judgement in the Sun*

1967   *The Flim-Flam Man* (Twentieth Century-Fox)
        aka: *One Born Every Minute*
        Hour of the Gun (Mirisch Corp.)
        Meanest Men in the West (Universal/Revue)
        The Ambushers (Columbia/Claude/Meadway)

1968   *Three Guns for Texas* (Universal)

1971   *Escape from the Planet of the Apes* (Twentieth Century-
        Fox/APJAC)
        Lawman (United Artists/Scimitar Films)
        Something Big (Stanmore/Penbar/Cinema Center 100)
        The Deserter (Dina de Laurentiis/Heritage/Jadran)
        aka: *La Spina dorsale del diavolo*

aka: *Djavolja kicma*
aka: *Ride to Glory*

1972   *Female Artillery* (Universal)
            The Manhunter (Universal)
            Kung Fu (Warner Brothers)

1974   *The Crazy World of Julius Vrooder* (Twentieth Century-Fox/Playboy)
            A Place Without Parents
            aka: *Truckin'*
            The Legend of Earl Durand (Howco)
            Night Games (Paramount)
            The Take (World Film)

1977   *Empire of the Ants* (Cinema 77)
            Black Oak Conspiracy (Vint/Clark)
            Moonshine County Express (New World Pictures)
            aka: *Shine*
            Viva Knievel! (Metropolitan)
            aka: *Seconds to Live*

1978   *Sweet Creek County War* (Imagery Films)

1979   *Love and Bullets* (Incorporated TV Co/Sir Lew Grade)
            Undercover with the KKK (Columbia)
            aka: *The Freedom Riders*
            aka: *My Undercover Years with the KKK*

1980   *Brubaker* (Twentieth Century-Fox)
            Steel (Fawcett-Majors/Steel)
            aka: *Look Down and Die*
            aka: *Men of Steel*
            Caddyshack (Orion)
            Cloud Dancer (Simon/Brown)
            Cuba Crossing (Jack White/Key West)
            aka: *Assignment: Kill Castro*
            aka: *Key West Crossing*

aka: *Kill Castro*
aka: *The Mercenaries*
aka: *Sweet Dirty Tony*
aka: *Sweet Violent Tony*
The Great Cash Giveaway Getaway (Papazian)
aka: *The Magnificent Hustle*
Portrait of a Rebel: The Remarkable Mrs. Sanger (Haywood)
aka: *Portrait of a Rebel: Margaret Sanger*

1981   *Dragonslayer* (Paramount/Disney)
Guns and Fury
St. Helens (Davis-Panzer)
aka: *St. Helens, Killer Volcano*
Burned at the Stake (Landsburg)
aka: *The Coming*

1982   *I'm Dancing as Fast as I Can* (Paramount)
Love Child (The Ladd Co.)
Superstition (Carolco/Panaria)
aka: *The Witch*
Thou Shalt Not Kill (Warner Brothers)

1984   *Hard to Hold* (Universal)
Best Kept Secrets (ABC/Sarabande)
Fatal Vision (NBC)

1986   *Dress Gray* (NBC)
Born American (Cinema Group/Larmark/Man & Gun/
Videogramm)
aka: *Arctic Heat*
aka: *Jäätävä polte*

1988   *Jesse* (Republic)

1989   *Billy the Kid* (Von Zerneck Sertner Films)
Breaking In (Act III/Breaking In/Samuel Goldwyn)

TV SERIES & MINI-SERIES

1964-5	*Daniel Boone*
1974-6	*Petrocelli*
1976	*Once an Eagle*, mini-series
1977	*Harold Robbins' 79 Park Avenue*, mini-series
1978	*Greatest Heroes of the Bible*, mini-series

TELEVISION

1954   *Danger* – "The Little Woman"

1956   *The U.S. Steel Hour* – "Survival"
The U.S. Steel Hour – "Noon on Doomsday"
The U.S. Steel Hour – "Bang the Drum Slowly"
Studio One – "The Open Door"

1957   *Alfred Hitchcock Presents* – "The Dangerous People"
The U.S. Steel Hour – "The Hill Wife"
Kraft Theatre – "Most Blessed Woman"
Kaiser Aluminum Hour – "So Short a Season"

1958   *Alfred Hitchcock Presents* – "The Jokester"
Climax – "The Volcano Seat"
Westinghouse Studio One – "Man Under Glass"

1959   *Adventures in Paradise* – "Somewhere South of Suva"
G.E. Theatre – "The Family Man"

1960   *Have Gun Will Travel* – "Vernon Good"/"The Sanctuary"
Rawhide – "Incident of the Captive"
Bonanza – "Silent Thunder"
Hotel de Paree – "Sundance and the Delayed Gun"
One Step Beyond – "The Peter Hurkos Story", parts 1 & 2
The Twilight Zone – "Execution"

1961   *Naked City* – "Button in the Haystack"
        Play of the Week – "The Old Foolishness"
        Wagon Train – "Wagon to Fort Anderson"
        The Untouchables – "Power Play"
        Tales of Wells Fargo – "Jeremiah"
        The Investigators – "Panic Wagon"
        The Twilight Zone – "A Quality of Mercy"

1962   *The Defenders* – "The Apostle"
        Stoney Burke – "The Wanderer"
        Combat! – "Cat and Mouse"
        The Virginian – "It Tolls for Thee"
        The Eleventh Hour – "Angie, You Made My Heart Stop"
        Saints and Sinners – "Three Columns of Anger"
        Wagon Train – "The Frank Carter Story"
        Route 66 – "A Long Piece of Mischief"

1963   *Route 66* – "93% in Smiling"
        Redigo – "Man in a Blackout"
        The Virginian – "Brother Thaddeus"
        The Travels of Jamie McPheeters – "The Day of the First
        Suitor"
        Route 66 – "But Who Will Cheer My Bonny Bride?"
        Twilight Zone – "Of Late, I Think of Cliffordville"
        Rawhide – "Incident of the Pale Rider"
        Alfred Hitchcock Theatre – "I'll Be Judge, I'll Be Jury"
        Grand Slam – unsold pilot

1964   *Profiles in Courage* – "The Mary S. McDowell Story"
        Destry – "The Nicest Girl in Gomorrah"
        The Fugitive – "Angels Travel on Lonely Roads",
        Parts 1 & 2

1965   *Laredo* – "Jinx"
        I Spy – "Weight of the World"
        The Virginian – "A Little Learning"

1966	*12 O'clock High* – "The Pariah"
	T.H.E. Cat – "Brotherhood"
	Jericho – "Have Traitor, Will Travel"
	The Monroes – "Wild Dog of the Tetons"
	The F.B.I. – "The Plunderers"
	The Legend of Jesse James – "The Lonely Place"
	Voyage to the Bottom of the Sea – "Dead Man's Doubloons"
	The Big Valley – "Under a Dark Star"
	Lost in Space – "The Sky Pirate"
	Gunsmoke – "Death Watch"
	A Man Called Shenandoah – "The Accused"
1967	*The Big Valley* – "The Buffalo Man"
	Cimarron Strip – "The Last Wolf"
	Custer – "Dangerous Prey"
	Gentle Ben – "Knight of the Road"
	The Road West – "Elizabeth's Odyssey"
	Gunsmoke – "Mistaken Identity"
	Lost in Space – "Treasure of the Lost Planet"
1968	*That Girl* – "Great Guy"
	Judd for the Defense – "What Can You Do With Money?"
	Bonanza – "The Thirteenth Man"
	Gentle Ben – "'Gator Man"
	The Virginian – "The Death Wagon"
1970	*Hollywood Television Theatre* – "The Andersonville Trial"
	Gunsmoke – "Sergeant Holly"
	Hawaii Five-O – "The Payoff"
	San Francisco International Airport – "The High Cost of Nightmares"
	The Interns – "An Afternoon in the Fall"
	McCloud – "Murder Arena"
	aka: "The Concrete Corral"
	Land of the Giants – "Graveyard of Fools"
	World of Disney – "Menace on the Mountain", parts 1 & 2

1971   *The F.B.I.* – "Three-Way Split"
            The Name of the Game – "Showdown"
            High Chaparral – "A Man to Match the Land"

1972   *The F.B.I.* – "Canyon of No Return"
            Bonanza – "Ambush at Rio Lobo"
            Bonanza – "Search in Limbo"
            Night Gallery – "The Waiting Room"

1973   *Ironside* – "The Double-Edged Corner"
            Barnaby Jones – "The Deadly Prize"
            Hollywood Television Theatre – "Winesburg, Ohio"
            The Streets of San Francisco – "House on Hyde Street"
            Love, American Style – "Love and the Vertical Romance"
            Kung Fu – "Nine Lives"
            McMillan and Wife – "No Hearts, No Flowers"
            Ironside – "Ollinger's Last Case"

1974   *Kung Fu* – "Cry of the Night Beast"
            Police Story – "A Dangerous Age"
            Hec Ramsey – "Scar Tissue"
            Toma – "A Funeral for Max Berlin"

1975   *Theatre in America* – "Who's Happy Now?"

1976   *Tattletales*
            Ellery Queen – "The Adventure of the Tyrant of Tin Pan Alley"
            Run, Joe, Run – ep. 1/17/76

1977   *Police Story* – "The Six-Foot Stretch"
            McNamara's Band – series pilot 5/14/77
            McNamara's Band – second series pilot 12/5/77
            Future Cop – "The Mad, Mad Bomber"
            Baretta – "The Runaways"
            Insight – "Leroy"

1978	*James at Sixteen* – ep. 2/9/78
1979	*B.J. and the Bear* – "Shine On"
1980	*The Yeagers* – ep. 6/8/80
1981	*The Golden Age of Television* – "Bang the Drum Slowly" & interviews
1982	*St. Elsewhere* – "Legionnaires: Part 1"
	Dallas – "The Ewing Touch"
	Dallas – "Fringe Benefits"
	The Fall Guy – "Guess Who's Coming to Town"
1983	*Scarecrow & Mrs. King* – "The Long Christmas Eve"
	Hart to Hart – "Highland Fling"
	Knight Rider – "Custom K.I.T.T."
	The A-Team – "Diamonds 'n' Dust"
	Small and Frye – "The Case of the Concerned Husband"
	Ace Crawford, Private Eye – ep. 3/29/83
	Simon & Simon – "The Secret of the Chrome Eagle"
	Bring 'em Back Alive – "The Shadow Women of Chung Tai"
	Simon & Simon – "The Club Murder Vacation"
	Dallas – "Crash of '83"
1984	*Knots Landing* – "Love to Take You Home"
	Trapper John, MD – "Double Bubble"
1985	*Knots Landing* – "To Sing His Praise"
	Murder, She Wrote – "Murder Takes a Bus"
1989	*Mission: Impossible* – "The Fuhrer's Children"
	B-Men – unsold pilot
	The Young Riders – "Speak No Evil"

PLAYS

1949	*The Burning Bush*	Actor's Workshop theatre, NY
1951	*Squaring the Circle*	
1953	*Day of Grace*	Westport Stock
	Harvey	The Catskills
	The Male Animal	Fishkill Summer Theater, NY
	The Scarecrow	Off-Broadway
	End as a Man	Off-Broadway, then Broadway
1954	*A Month in the Country*	
	The Rainmaker	Broadway
1955	*Bus Stop*	Broadway, then national tour
1956	*The Good Woman of Setzuan*	Broadway
1958	*Howie*	Broadway
1959	*The Failures*	Broadway
1961	*Once There Was a Russian*	Broadway, DC & Delaware
1966	*Anna Christie*	Los Angeles
1968	*The Price*	Broadway, then London
1975	*Who's Happy Now?*	Los Angeles

Appendix I
Depression

"Oh, it can get rough, Mr. Helm, very rough."

– Albert Salmi as Jose Ortega/Leopold Caselius
The Ambushers

The National Institute of Mental Health tells us that, in America alone, over nineteen million people suffer from depressive illness each year. Depression is not confined to Americans, however. People all over the world share this problem. The Finnish seem to be especially susceptible to it. Many of the people who have suffered from depressive illness have names that are familiar to us: Mark Twain, Stephen Foster, Cole Porter, Alfred Lord Tennyson, Michelangelo, and Abraham Lincoln, to name but a few. The name of Albert Salmi can be added to this list of extremely gifted men.

Here are more sad statistics: Untreated depression is the number-one cause of suicide (seventy percent). The suicide rate for people with severe, untreated depression is around fifteen percent.

Such severe depression is in *no* way a sign of weakness, nor does it indicate a character flaw. It does, however, affect the entire body and mind in a way that can be devastating. It affects the way you eat and sleep, the way you feel about yourself, and your very thoughts.

Here are typical symptoms that are associated with depression:

- Persistent sad, anxious, or empty mood
- Feelings of hopelessness, pessimism, indifference
- Feelings of guilt, worthlessness, helplessness

- Loss of interest or pleasure in hobbies and activities that you once enjoyed, social withdrawal
- Insomnia, early-morning awakening, or over-sleeping
- Appetite and/or weight loss, or overeating and weight gain
- Decreased energy, fatigue, being "slowed down"
- Recurring thoughts of death or suicide, suicide attempts
- Restlessness, irritability
- Difficulty concentrating, remembering, making decisions
- Persistent, unexplained physical symptoms that do not respond to treatment, such as headaches, digestive disorders, and chronic pain

"It is hard to try to describe how depression feels," says Jennifer DeBost, a writer/artist who suffered from it for many years. "At times, you feel utterly hopeless, dark, desolate, despondent, like you are in a hole that is spiraling downward. You feel exhausted, numb, have no interests or appetites and no desire or energy to help yourself. During this time, you sleep constantly to avoid having to feel. At other times, there is rage, anger, and hatred for yourself, others, and the world in general, which is why suicide seems the only way out. Life obstacles seem insurmountable. Negativity is everywhere. Happiness seems like a foreign emotion that you can't remember and will never feel again."

Poet Rod McKuen recalls that awful time in his life. "When my depression took hold, I had a hard time even getting up in the morning. From the time I woke up to the time I struggled to get back to sleep it was as though there was a huge weight on my shoulders that I couldn't shake off. For months at a time I never left the house or the yard. Didn't answer mail or the telephone…. My depression took me completely down. I didn't get down on others or the world but I felt so inadequate and unable to cope that I certainly didn't want to be with people."

The book *Good Grief,* by Granger E. Westberg, describes it this way:

> This is what depression is like. Something seems to come between the person and God and between the person and his fellow men, so that he feels a tremendous loneliness, an awful sense of isolation. And he can't seem to break through it.
>
> When we are depressed, we find ourselves thinking thoughts we never have otherwise…

Later, the book continues,

> He is convinced that this is a state in which he will remain
> the rest of his life. Any attempt to try to convince him oth-
> erwise is useless.[1]

Not everyone suffering from depression will experience every symp-
tom. Some people have only a few; others have many. The severity of the
symptoms varies from person to person, ranging from short and mild to
long-term and life-threatening.

If these symptoms occur without a clear cause, when emotional reac-
tions are out of proportion to events, and especially when symptoms interfere
with day-to-day functioning, professional help should be obtained. One should
most definitely seek professional help if he is entertaining suicidal thoughts.

The first place one should go for help would be to a licensed, practicing psychologist (Ph.D. or Psy.D.) or a community mental health center or contracting affiliate. A psychologist is specially trained to recognize
and treat depression. This doctor may then refer his patient to a medical
doctor for a physical examination and, perhaps, medication.

A psychiatrist is a medical doctor who specializes in disorders that in-
volve the mind. He or she can prescribe medication and therapy that can
literally make the difference between life and death to a depressed individual.

Other sources of help for depressive illness:

- Local suicide hotlines
- Hospital emergency room
- Members of the clergy who are specially trained in men-
  tal-health issues

Environmental factors, as well as genetic and biochemical ones, all
work together to determine our emotional stability. Rev. Cecil Bolding,
EdD, LPC, of New Life Counseling Services, explained that there are
different types of depression:

"Situational depression," he says, is a phrase that some professionals
have coined to indicate the type of depression that occurs when something
in the person's environment caused the illness. This type is also called "reactive depression." Triggers could include such life-changing catastrophes as

---

1. Reprinted by permission from *Good Grief* by Granger E. Westberg, © 1997 Augsburg Fortress.

the death of a child, the loss of a job, or divorce. Therapy is usually the treatment of choice in this case. In many instances, group therapy has proven quite beneficial. Other people are more responsive to individual therapy. If the situation causing the depression is abuse of some kind, prompt removal of the person from the unhealthy environment is, of course, crucial.

"Clinical depresson," on the other hand, is biological in nature. This is treated with medication, along with therapy. Research has proven that the combination of medication and psychotherapy offers the most effective treatment for depression. With appropriate treatment, over eighty percent of sufferers can find relief.

The National Depressive and Manic-Depressive Association states that reactive depression may become clinical depression if the symptoms last for over two weeks. Either type, it says, is indicative of an imbalance of the brain chemicals called neurotransmitters.

Dr. Bolding stressed that when one's treatment involves taking an antidepressant, it is extremely important to avoid all forms of alcohol. Alcohol, a depressant itself, would counteract the medication, rendering it useless, at best. At worst, the combination of such medication and alcohol could be lethal.

Unfortunately, Albert did not seek appropriate help for his depression. The attempted sexual exploitation by a psychiatrist of an acquaintance of Albert's many years earlier had left him with a permanent distrust of all psychiatrists. Right when he needed such help desperately, he had no one to turn to. So instead of receiving appropriate medication and/or therapy to alleviate the symptoms of his depression, he chose to self-medicate with alcohol and Placidyl, a habit-forming sleeping pill that he and Roberta had both been using for years. Jenny said that these sleeping pills had been sent to her parents in bottles of five hundred from a doctor in Los Angeles, even though it is known to cause both psychological and physical dependence. Because it's such an addictive drug, most doctors have weaned their patients off of Placidyl and stopped prescribing it. Some pharmacies haven't carried this drug for years. An attorney later advised Jenny that Placidyl had been known to cause psychotic behavior, as well. In any event, alcohol and sleeping pills are both "downers" and did nothing to relieve Albert's depression.

Albert ran out of Placidyl in March, and went off of it "cold turkey." As a result of this, he probably suffered from sleep deprivation, in addition to depression.

What his daughters wish they had known at the time was that there is much that family members can do to help someone who is suffering from depressive illness:

- Express concern for the pain, physical and emotional, that your loved one is experiencing. Take him seriously.
- Be specific. Tell him exactly what it is about his behavior or circumstances that distresses you.
- Do what you can to ease his guilty feelings, while letting him know that those troubling feelings are symptoms of a *treatable* illness.
- Be candid with professionals and others who can help your loved one. Do what you can to help them help him. Don't keep confidential any information that may save his life.
- Let your loved one know, in specific terms, how devastating his suicide would be to you and others.
- If he is hospitalized, visit him, maintain communication with his doctor, and don't put pressure on them to release him before his in-patient treatment is completed.

More information about depression is available at the Depression and Bi-Polar Support Alliance, website www.ndmda.org, phone (800) 826-3632, and the American Foundation for Suicide Prevention, website www.afsp.org, phone (888) 333-2377.

Appendix II
The Impact Albert Salmi Made On His Fans

"I wouldn't dream of depriving you of my company."

– Albert Salmi as Sgt. Jenkins
Combat! Episode "Cat and Mouse"

If you had encountered Albert on the street, what would you have said? Do you think you would shake his hand and thank him for the wonderful entertainment he provided for so many years? What did most people say when they saw him in person for the first time?

Lizanne says, "I remember that people would come up to him and tell him that they thought they knew him, but they didn't know where from. Sometimes they would say, 'Are you an actor?' I think that once he told someone that yes, he was an actor—Albert Salmi—and they didn't believe him!"

We can just envision it, can't we? It probably went something like this:

"Are you an actor?" asks TV viewer, scratching his head.

"Yes, I am. My name is Albert Salmi."

TV viewer smirks, sure that he's being conned. "Albert Salmi? Aw, come on. Who are you *really?*"

Such is the lot of a character actor, especially such a good one. On his What-a-Character website, David Mazor defined character actors as "The names you don't remember, the faces you can't forget." He hit the nail right on the head!

Some people made a point to remember Albert's name, however. "He did get a lot of fan mail from all over," Lizanne continued. "He got mail from

Canada, Russia, Germany—you wouldn't believe the places he got mail from. I have to say that he wasn't that great at replying to fan mail, at least in Spokane. He might have been better about it in L.A. because I think my mom helped him and possibly his agent." If you ever wrote Albert a fan letter, though, you can rest assured that he did read it. The only fan letters that he did not read were those received after February, 1990. It says much for his staying power and effectiveness as an actor that, at age sixty-two and semi-retired after forty years in the business, Albert was still receiving fan mail.

As is true of anything else, his viewers perceived Albert in different ways. Some of his fans were simply in awe of his dramatic performances in such emotional productions as *The U.S. Steel Hour*'s "Bang the Drum Slowly" and *The Brothers Karamazov*. To many others, he was associated chiefly with westerns, usually as the bad guy or the sheriff. Still others favored his more quirky or unusual characters.

"He was always very popular here in Australia," says stage actor Ric Tester of Sydney. "I was mesmerized by his performance. He paid great attention to the finest details of his performance—the eye movements, the subtle changes of facial expression and the body language were all so expertly reflective of the characters he portrayed."

Ric continues, "Early in 1999, I played the role of baddie Jud Fry in the stage show *Oklahoma*. Traditionally, Jud has been done as a very one-dimensional, brutish character, but I thought that I would try to bring something new to the role. I thought, 'How would Albert Salmi have done this?' I looked at quite a few of his works on video . . . and then used my imagination and came up with a character who was bad, but who was still a human being. I did my best at copying Albert's oft-used slow and deliberate speech pattern. The whole thing went quite well, judging from some of the positive comments I received."

Sheldon Berger has been a fan for many years. "When I was young," he says, "my late father and I used to see who could guess the character actor appearing on TV at the moment, and Albert Salmi was one of our favorites. He could be pretty sinister at times, and we just loved his voice." He added, "Of course, my dad said, 'Look! It's Albert Salami!' but, to a fourteen-year-old, that can be funny, especially in 1960."

"Albert Salmi was terrific in both of the episodes he appeared in on *Lost in Space*," says fan Steve Tanner. "I was very young when the show initially aired, but his character of Captain Tucker really made an impression on me and has stayed with me through the years. It brings back great feelings from my childhood whenever I watch *Lost in Space*, especially when it's an episode like 'The Sky Pirate,' with Albert Salmi. That particular episode is one of the most memorable from my childhood. When watching it again for the first time in years, I could remember EVERYTHING that was about to happen, proving that I paid very close attention as a kid."

In 1999, an informal poll was conducted over the internet. Fans were asked four questions:

1. What did you like about Albert Salmi, the person and the actor?
2. What did you dislike about him?
3. What do you feel was his most memorable performance?
4. With which kind of character do you most identify him— bad guy, authority figure, or misunderstood good guy?

The answers were quite varied. Here is what they said:

What You Like

"He was always 'down to earth;' seemed like someone easy to talk to, approachable, unpretentious. He was believable in his roles."

"He never appeared to be acting. You could believe he was whatever role he played."

"He really stood out in a group—no matter where or how many others were around, he stood out in a crowd. A commanding presence. When he wasn't playing a bad guy, he was often playing a role of 'everyman'—very appealing. One other thing—he was so versatile (westerns, contemporary comedies or dramas, sci-fi stuff) that you never knew where he might turn up. But it was always a pleasure when he did."

"I like the intensity he brought to his roles."

"It was a combo of versatility in playing different characters well, and also a plain ol' attraction to his rugged masculinity and harsh Nordic features."

"Honestly—I know nothing of the person, only the actor; and he seems quite good. I remember him chiefly as a loud-mouthed type villain who typically I couldn't stand but who adequately portrayed whatever misdeed or villainy needed to be for the sake of the storyline."

"I didn't know the man, but the actor was grand. He was so believable in all his roles. He played characters that you just didn't like. Not every actor can pull that off consistently. He was always kind of on the edge. You liked not liking the character he portrayed."

"I have always loved his voice…one of the things that makes him and his body of work very memorable. I remember always wanting to see TV eps he was in, even if I didn't care for the series, because he was such a good actor. He so often made me angry at him. The hallmark of a superb actor. Then, when he portrayed someone with a heart, I felt guilty for not liking him in other series! The *Combat* ep still bothers me. I react the same way Sgt. Saunders does—(paraphrasing here: I never disliked a man so much so quickly, but I will never be able to forget him)."

What You Dislike

"Can't say!"

"Can't think of anything."

"Only that, for a great portion of his career, he seemed to have been typecast as the 'heavy'—usually a bad guy in a uniform or a bad guy out to get the guys in uniform. From gunslinger to guard, he was most known for his bad-guy roles. I suppose if a casting director was looking for a southern-sounding bad guy, he would probably be one of the first actors considered."

"Sometimes he made me 'dislike' him through a great portrayal of a dislikable character."

"Nothing really—sometimes he had a slimy-type look I didn't like, but usually fit the part."

Most Memorable Role

"Probably Yadkin [in the television series *Daniel Boone*]; other appearances were mostly guest appearances of what I saw. This role provided consistent exposure."

"In *The U.S. Steel Hour* production, 1956, of 'Bang the Drum Slowly'."

"Yadkin may have been his most memorable role—his role in *Petrocelli* probably brought him more actual exposure and publicity among the general population, but still not memorable. (I still can't remember the character's name!)…if Yadkin has survived over 30 years in my mind, then yes, it was his most memorable role. However, some of his television appearances that stand out in my mind—*Gunsmoke, Combat, Big Valley* (the good-guy role, not the bad guard!), *Bonanza, Love American Style, That Girl, The Andersonville Trial, Voyage to the Bottom of the Sea.*"

"Can't remember the name of it—just have this image of him mouthing off some orders to someone—maybe it was the *Combat* episode 'Cat and Mouse'."

"Yadkin, of course! I liked him most in the westerns, though he did well in the science fiction area, too."

"Of all the random whirling memories in my head, I always remember him in *Wild River* and [*Bonanza*'s] 'Silent Thunder'."

"I think that his performance in the *Combat!* episode entitled 'Cat and Mouse' was the best. He was an egotistical know-it-all, but he laid down his life for Sgt. Saunders, who had come to hate the guy. Ironically, Saunders returns with the info and the sad tale of Salmi's character's death, but the info is not needed any longer and no one seems to care about Salmi or his death. It's one of the few performances where viewers sympathize with Salmi's character, even though viewers weren't meant to like him."

"I think what I remember him best for was when he was on *Daniel Boone*. I really liked his character on there."

"*Rawhide*—one of the later seasons—don't know the title, but he played a man who had been buried alive and survived. The burial may have been an attempt to fake his death, as he was a wanted man. He came after Rowdy Yates, over and over, calling him 'Mr. Ramrod,' wanting him dead, and blaming him for making the burial necessary. I don't remember much more than that, except it was very spooky." [The title of that episode was "Incident of the Pale Rider."]

Character Identification

"Yadkin."

"I'd say, if I had to choose between those three, the third one." [misunderstood good guy]

"He was everywhere—you couldn't pin him down in any one role."

"Even though he was most memorable as Yadkin (a case of first impression being the strongest, maybe?), I think he made a baaaaaaad bad guy! Really gave me the shivers!"

"Definitely bad guy."

"BAD EVIL SINISTER guy…Always a villain!"

"Although he did play the bad guy well, I like him as the sidekick or the trapper/hunter characters. He just seemed to have the body and soul for those characters."

"I think of him mainly as a narrow-minded, prejudiced, egotistical man who won't or can't see the wider picture. Regardless of whether or not he was the heavy—like in a *Streets of San Francisco* episode where he simply played the father of a child involved with breaking and entering a house of two old brothers—he portrayed characters that viewers just didn't like. I admire a man who so consistently played characters like that. It must have taken great security and confidence in his personal life and knowing who he really and truly was to take that chance. I always thought I'd like to have met him."

Other Comments

"I was very sad and surprised when I heard of his death. Stunned actually."

"Just that it was a shock when I only recently learned that he had died (violently) several years ago. I wondered why I hadn't heard about it before now (it was just a month ago that I learned of his death). I thought about him all that weekend, don't now why—I never met the man. It was just so shocking and upsetting. I still look forward to seeing him in his roles, though. Also, I was surprised to learn that he wasn't a southern boy—he sure had me fooled all these years!"

"I've seen him for years in so many things."

"I've enjoyed his work over the years, from *The Brothers Karamazov* to the classic TV series *Alcoa Presents One Step Beyond.*"

"His presence was felt and I always thought he could have been a backwoodsman in real life. Whether he liked to do that kind of thing, I don't know. But he put the realism into his character."

"I always enjoyed the *Daniel Boone*s with him in them."

"I saw a movie a couple weeks ago, where Albert portrayed a bench judge…and he said 'Well now…' I didn't catch the beginning, but when I heard his voice, my mind went 'Yad!' So I watched it from that point on."

*   *   *

Albert appreciated his fans, too. Lizanne says, "I remember that when he would visit me at work at The Crescent Department Store in Spokane, people were thrilled to see him. He was very nice to everyone that I worked with."

Index

Lightning Source UK Ltd.
Milton Keynes UK
UKHW02f0633300518
323444UK00011B/675/P